The Owl
and
the Nightingale

The Lockert Library Of Poetry In Translation

SERIES EDITORS
Peter Cole, Richard Sieburth, and Rosanna Warren

SERIES EDITOR EMERITUS (1991–2016)
Richard Howard

For other titles in the Lockert Library, see the list at the end of this volume.

The Owl
and
the Nightingale

A NEW VERSE TRANSLATION

Simon Armitage

PRINCETON UNIVERSITY PRESS
PRINCETON AND OXFORD

Published by Princeton University Press
41 William Street, Princeton, New Jersey 08540
99 Banbury Road, Oxford OX2 6JX

press.princeton.edu

First published in Great Britain in different form by Faber and Faber.

First Princeton paperback printing, 2024
Paperback ISBN 9780691206189

The Library of Congress has cataloged the cloth edition as follows:

Names: Armitage, Simon, 1963– translator.
Title: The owl and the nightingale / a new verse translation [by] Simon Armitage.
Other titles: Owl and the nightingale (Middle English poem)
Description: Princeton, New Jersey : Princeton University Press, [2022] | Series: The Lockert library of poetry in translation
Identifiers: LCCN 2021035941 | ISBN 9780691202167 (hardback)
Subjects: LCSH: Birds—Poetry. | Debate poetry, English (Middle) | Debate poetry, English (Middle)—Translations into English. | LCGFT: Debate poetry.
Classification: LCC PR2109.O7 A317 2022 | DDC 821/.1—dc23
LC record available at https://lccn.loc.gov/2021035941

British Library Cataloging-in-Publication Data is available

Editorial: Anne Savarese and James Collier
Production Editorial: Ellen Foos
Text and Jacket/Cover Design: Pamela L. Schnitter
Production: Erin Suydam
Publicity: Jodi Price
Copyeditor: Jennifer Harris

Jacket/Cover art (spine): Composite of (1) Detail of a miniature of an owl being mobbed by other birds; from a bestiary, England, 13th century. Harley MS 4751, f. 47r. © The British Library; (2) A bird of prey hovering over a duck under water, England (probably Glastonbury), ca. 1400–1410. Harley 7026, f. 16r. © The British Library

The Lockert Library of Poetry in Translation is supported by a bequest from Charles Lacy Lockert (1999–1974)

This book has been composed in Adobe Text Pro

CONTENTS

INTRODUCTION

A narrator describes entering a remote valley in summer, where an owl and a nightingale are engaged in a bitter disagreement. It is a quarrel that continues for the better part of eighteen hundred lines of verse, in a style or genre sometimes described as "comic debate poetry," and although the poetry is indeed comic and even hilarious on occasions, the word "debate" lends a tone of intellectual politeness to what is at times a medieval slanging match. The fact that the birds are conversing in the language of humans is never explained or excused, and our unwitting acceptance of this situation from beginning to end can be taken as a confirmation of poetic achievement.

Of the many mysterious poems to have survived from the Middle Ages, *The Owl and the Nightingale* is one of the most mysterious of all. Despite expert investigation and analysis from many different angles, its date of composition is still a matter of speculation, with almost a hundred years separating the earlier and later possibilities. At lines 1091 and 1092 of the manuscript, the nightingale invokes the name of "King Henri," adding, "Jesus his soule do merci." The reference implies that the king is dead, but is this Henry II, who died in 1189, or Henry III, who wore the crown for fifty-six years until passing away in 1279? Two other monarchs occupied the throne during that period; the idea that the poem can't be confidently assigned to a particular reign, let alone a year or even a decade, seems to darken its shadowy beginnings. "A twelfth- or thirteenth-century poem" is often how *The Owl and the Nightingale* is described.

Dating the poem's original composition would be easier if we knew who wrote it, but we don't. One candidate is a Master Nicholas of Guildford, a resident of Portesham in Dorset apparently, who is mentioned on two occasions in the poem as a man of sound judgment, someone who might objectively settle the dispute between the warring birds. Indeed, the flawlessness of his character is one of the few things the birds are able to agree on. However, if it seems to make sense that a named person within the poem is likely to be its author, it seems just as likely to me that the author could be deflecting attention away from his own identity, or even sending up a third party with sycophantic praise. In this translation, I have replaced Master Nicholas with the name of a poet who has a more reliable connection with the text. Further to the subject of authorship, I have referred to the narrator and the poet as "he" in this introduction, but only through a sense of informed speculation based on the literary norms and precedents of the era. And interestingly, both the owl and the nightingale of the poem are female.

If authorship were established, this might help throw light on the geographical origins of the poem (and vice versa), but on this topic, too, there is no consensus of opinion. The analysis of vocabulary, dialect words, and regional spellings in Middle English poems often helps to pinpoint, or at least narrow down, their place of composition. In the case of *The Owl and the Nightingale*, locations as far apart as Kent and the West Midlands have been proposed, as well as Wessex—an area that would include most of Britain's southern coast and parts of the South West.

Uncertainty in regard to all those issues both reflects and reinforces hesitancy about the poem's ultimate meaning. Clearly the birds, with their personalities, habits, abilities, and physical characteristics, are representatives of particular ways of life and philosophical outlooks. This is especially true in relation to their Christian faith, and many critical commentaries focus on the extent to which the birds draw on biblical teaching to provide their themes and support their arguments. However, their individual claims to a religious and moral high ground are often undermined by contradictions in logic and descents into decidedly un-Christian rancor. The fact that their dispute remains unresolved at the end of the poem (despite the intervention of a wren, and with several other species of bird turning up to lend muscle or opinion) only adds to the ambiguity surrounding the author's intentions. That said, poetry of historical eras is always of more interest when it seems relevant and relatable to the contemporary reader, and on this front *The Owl and the Nightingale* does not disappoint. The dialogue between the birds resonates with issues that preoccupy latter-day society, including matters of identity, culture, the right to be heard, and class distinctions. The superior tones of the nightingale clash and contrast with the more pragmatic attitudes of the owl, the song of one trying to win out over the screech of the other. Questions of personal hygiene, toilet habits, parenting skills, dietary preferences, and sexual conduct also enter their bickering, alongside more elevated disagreements on the themes of individuality, survival, community, and conscience, all traded in uncompromising, adversarial terms. If the poem was designed as an allegorical pastiche of humanity's predilection for vitriolic disagreement, then the two birds would not be out of place several centuries later, wrestling for "control of the narrative" in an internet chat-room or across social media platforms.

But if the poem's overall significance remains elusive, what is not in doubt is the quality of the writing or, more specifically, its poetics. To produce a work of nearly nine hundred rhyming couplets written in near-regular meter (iambic tetrameter) requires stamina and patience. It also insists on an exceptional level of creative ingenuity if the poem is to stay agile and alert from beginning to end. There is great inventiveness on display here, and the kind of authorial self-awareness and subtlety that distinguishes literature from mere information, and transforms the studied documentation of an idea into something we call art.

There are two surviving manuscripts, one held by the British Library (MS Cotton Caligula A.ix (C), ff. 233ra–246ra) and one held by Jesus College, Oxford (MS 29 (J), ff. 156ra–168vb), both thought to have been copied from a single original or "exemplar," now lost. Nuanced differences between the two versions are a matter of great importance and excitement to scholars of the poem; they are of less concern in this translation, though for the most part I have followed the British Library version.

I have described my working processes, and my reasons for taking on these old anonymous poems, and my interest in medieval poetry generally, in introductions to other translations and in published lectures. But experience tells me that for the everyday reader, perhaps picking this book off the bookshelf out of idle curiosity (and thank you, if you have), one question comes to the fore. How can English be translated into English? I hope that question can be answered relatively quickly by quoting the first four lines of the original poem, which read as follows:

Ich was in one summer dale
In one suþe diȝele hale
Iherde ich holde grete tale
An hule and one niȝtingale

Middle English can be very crudely characterized as a form of English spoken and written in Britain from the arrival of William the Conqueror (1066) to the first printed editions of Chaucer's *Canterbury Tales* (1476). The Middle English alphabet included the two letters thorn (þ—similar in this instance to "th") and yogh (ȝ—similar in this instance to "gh"), now obsolete. Knowing how to pronounce those letters allows a twenty-first-century reader to give voice to passages in the poem and develop a reasonable sense of what is being said. But line two is tricky because it contains words we no longer use and whose definitions are somewhat blurred, even to experts. The word hale (corner? place? location? hollow? glade?) isn't going to earn its keep in a contemporary rendition, so immediately a new rhyming couplet is called for, which will inevitably require changes to preceding words. Medieval sentence structure presents as archaic to modern ears, so a certain amount of grammatical reshaping is also necessary. And some words, even if they have retained their inherent meaning over several hundred years, have often acquired new and sometimes unhelpful connotations, just as some modern words might feel anachronistic or out of place, no matter how accurate their definitions. Add to this the need to position words at particular locations in a line to conform to the prescribed rhythm of the poem, and something of the nature and scale of the task can be imagined.

It is interesting to speculate that seven or eight hundred years ago, all the uncertainties surrounding the poem as I have described them were probably not uncertainties at all, but very obvious facts. Except, that is, for the skill and verve of the author, who seems to have produced a work of unprecedented craft and virtuosic style in excess of the literary achievements of the period. Whatever audiences the poem reached, as readers or listeners they must have been mightily impressed by its theoretical inquiries and commanding use of language, and greatly entertained by its two main characters, whose verbal sniping and sparring has the authenticity of actual speech. If the poem is erudite and articulate, it is also idiomatic and at times vulgar, drawing on everyday experiences, deploying colloquial registers, and appealing to our common understanding of human behavior, albeit ventriloquized through the voices of two birds. The poem is almost a play, with an owl and a nightingale vying for the spotlight, and ultimately it is the theatrical and dramatic qualities of their monologues that I have attempted to capture and replicate in this translation.

The Owl
and
the Nightingale

Ich was in one sumere dale,
in one suþe diʒele hale,
iherde ich holde grete tale
an hule and one niʒtingale.
Þat plait was stif & starc & strong,
sum wile softe & lud among;
an aiþer aʒen oþer sval,
& let þat [vue]le mod ut al.
& eiþer seide of oþeres custe
þat alre-worste þat hi wuste:
& hure & hure of oþere[s] songe
hi holde plaiding suþe stronge.

Þe niʒtingale bigon þe speche,
in one hurne of one breche,
& sat up one vaire boʒe,
—þar were abute blosme inoʒe,—
in ore waste þicke hegge
imeind mid spire & grene segge.
Ho was þe gladur uor þe rise,
& song auele cunne wise:
[b]et þuʒte þe dreim þat he were
of harpe & pipe þan he nere:
bet þuʒte þat he were ishote
of harpe & pipe þan of þrote.

[Þ]o stod on old stoc þar biside,
þar þo vle song hire tide,
& was mid iui al bigrowe;
hit was þare hule earding-stowe.

2

One summer's day I overheard
a mighty war of words disturb
a peaceful & secluded dale;
between an Owl & Nightingale
barbed comments flew, now soft, now loud,
but always heartfelt, wounding, proud.
The birds, both swollen up with anger,
hurled abuse at one another,
taking turns to slate & curse
what in the other bird was worst,   10
with insults being especially strong
when rubbishing the other's song.

The Nightingale took up proceedings
from the corner of a clearing,
perching on a handsome bough
with blossoms hanging down & round,
beside a densely knotted hedge
entwined with reeds & bright green sedge.
She gloried in that branch; it formed
a kind of stage, & she performed   20
the music of her repertoire
as if she played a pipe or harp,
as if each bright, melodious note
were not the product of a throat.

There was, nearby, a tree-stump where
the Owl intoned her hourly prayers,
an ancient ivy-covered bole
the Owl had claimed as her abode.

[Þ]e niʒtingale hi iseʒ,
& hi bihold & ouerseʒ,   30
& þuʒte wel [vu]l of þare hule,
for me hi halt lodlich & fule.
"Vnwiʒt," ho sede, "awei þu flo!
me is þe w[u]rs þat ich þe so.
Iwis for þine [vu]le lete,
wel [oft ich] mine song forlete;
min horte atfliþ & falt mi tonge,
wonne þu art [to me] iþrunge.
Me luste bet speten þane singe
of þine fule ʒoʒelinge."   40

Þos hule abod fort hit was eve,
ho ne miʒte no leng bileue,
vor hire horte was so gret
þat wel neʒ hire fnast atschet,
& warp a word þar-after longe;
"Hu þincþe nu bi mine songe?
We[n]st þu þat ich ne cunne singe,
þeʒ ich ne cunne of writelinge?
Ilome þu dest me grame,
& seist me [boþe tone] & schame.   50
ʒif ich þe holde on mine uote,
(so hit bitide þat ich mote!)
& þu were vt of þine rise,
þu sholdest singe an oþer w[i]se."

Þe niʒtingale ʒaf answare:
"ʒif ich me loki wit þe bare,

4

The Nightingale clapped eyes on her
& shot the Owl a filthy glare,   30
disgusted by that horrid creature's
loathsome, nauseating features.
"Freak, why don't you disappear?
It sickens me to see you here.
Your ugly presence guarantees
to throw my fluting out of key.
In fact whenever you turn up
my jaw locks & my heart won't pump.
As for your tuneless yodeling
it makes me want to spit, not sing."   40

The Owl was silent until dusk,
by which time she was on the cusp
of rage, her lungs about to burst
through holding back her angry words,
her heart about to pop. She yowled,
"How does my music strike you now?
You tell yourself that I can't sing
but I'm not one for twittering.
You ridicule me & you mock,
snipe from the cover of the copse,   50
but if you flew that branch of yours
I'd make you welcome in my claws
(bring on that day before too long!)
& then you'd sing a different song!"

At which the Nightingale remarked,
"As long as I'm alert & sharp

5

& me schilde wit þe blete,
ne reche ich noȝt of þine þrete;
ȝif ich me holde in mine hegge,
ne recche ich neuer what þu segge.   60
Ich wot þat þu art unmilde
wiþ hom þat ne muȝe from [þ]e schilde;
& þu tukest wroþe & vuele,
whar þu miȝt, over smale fuȝele.
Vorþi þu art loþ al fuel-kunne,
& alle ho þe driueþ honne,
& þe bischricheþ & bigredet,
& wel narewe þe biledet;
& ek forþe þe sulue mose,
hire þonkes, wolde þe totose.   70
þu art lodlich to biholde,
& þu art loþ in monie volde;
þi bodi is short, þi swore is smal,
grettere is þin heued þan þu al;
þin eȝene boþ col-blake & brode,
riȝt swo ho weren ipeint mid wode;
þu starest so þu wille abiten
al þat þu mi[ȝ]t mid cliure smiten:
þi bile is stif & scharp & hoked,
riȝt so an owel þat is croked;   80
þar-mid þu clackes[t] oft & longe,
& þat is on of þine songe.
Ac þu þretest to mine fleshe,
mid þine cliures woldest me meshe.
þe were icundur to one frogge
snailes, mus, & fule wiȝte,

in open ground or on the wing
your menace has a hollow ring.
As long as I keep to the hedge
your words are simply worthless threats.   *60*
I've seen the ruthless way you rip
those birds who can't escape your grip,
& how you like to sink your pincers
into little larks & finches.
That's why feathered creatures hate you,
drive you from their patch, berate you
with their screams & cries, & why
they rise & mob you when you fly,
& why the tiniest of tits
would gladly tear you bit from bit.   *70*
You really are a gruesome sight
in ways too many to describe:
your neck's too thin, your trunk's too small,
your head is bigger than . . . your all!
Your coal-black eyes are weirdly broad
& look like they've been daubed with woad,
& glare as if you'd like to feast
on anyone within your reach.
Your bill is sharp & bent & hard—
a flesh-hook with a buckled barb—   *80*
that issues—loud & all day long—
some caterwaul you call a song.
You threaten me, & say your feet
will catch & mulch me into meat;
a frog, though, underneath the mill-wheel,
surely makes a truer Owl meal?

boþ þine cunde & þine riȝte.
Þu sittest adai & fliȝ[s]t aniȝt,
þu cuþest þat þu art on vnwiȝt.
Þu art lodlich & unclene,
bi þine neste ich hit mene,
& ek bi þine fule brode,
þu fedest on hom a wel ful fode.
Vel wostu þat hi doþ þarinne,
hi fuleþ hit up to þe chinne:
ho sitteþ þar so hi bo bisne.
Þarbi men segget a uorbisne:
'Dahet habbe þat ilke best
þat fuleþ his owe nest.'
Þat oþer ȝer a faukun bredde;
his nest noȝt wel he ne bihedde:
þarto þu stele in o dai,
& leidest þaron þi fole ey.
Þo hit bicom þat he haȝte,
& of his eyre briddes wraȝte;
ho broȝte his briddes mete,
bihold his nest, iseȝ hi ete:
he iseȝ bi one halue
his nest ifuled uthalue.
Þe faucun was wroþ wit his bridde,
& lude ȝal & sterne chidde:
'Segget me, wo hauet þis ido?
Ov nas neuer icunde þarto:
hit was idon ov a loþ[e] [cu]ste.
Segge[þ] me ȝif ȝe hit wiste.'

90

100

110

8

Snail & mouse & squelchy slug
are more your right & proper grub.
You roost by day & fly by night
which proves that something isn't right.   90
You are repellent & impure,
you & those filthy chicks of yours,
that brood of dirty-looking pests
you're raising in a filthy nest.
They soil the den they're living in
until their droppings reach their chins
then stand about as if they're blind,
which brings this truism to mind:
'Accursed be the wretched beast
that makes its toilet where it feeds.'   100
One year a falcon left her brood
& in her absence from the wood
you slipped into the clutch to lay
your ugly-looking egg one day,
& after several weeks had passed
& several of her chicks had hatched
she brought her young ones meat to eat
but noticed as the fledglings ate
that one half of the nest was neat,
the other in a squalid state.   110
The bird was livid with her young,
who felt the rough edge of her tongue.
'Explain who made this shameful mess.
No child of mine would foul the nest.
You're victims of a sneaky trick,
so tell me who committed it.'

9

Þo quaþ þat on & quad þat oþer:
'Iwis it was ure oȝer broþer,
þe ȝond þat haue[þ] þat grete heued:
wai þat hi[t] nis þarof bireued!   *120*
Worp hit ut mid þe alre-[vu]rste
þat his necke him to-berste!'
Þe faucun ilefde his bridde,
& nom þat fule brid amidde,
& warp hit of þan wilde bowe,
þar pie & crowe hit todrowe.
Herbi men segget a bispel,
þeȝ hit ne bo fuliche spel;
al so hit is bi þan ungode
þat is icumen of fule brode,   *130*
& is meind wit fro monne,
euer he cuþ þat he com þonne,
þat he com of þan adel-eye,
þeȝ he a fro nest[e] leie.
þeȝ appel trendli fro[m] þon trowe,
þar he & oþer mid growe,
þeȝ he bo þar-from bicume,
he cuþ wel whonene he is icume."

Þos word aȝaf þe niȝtingale,
& after þare longe tale   *140*
he song so lude & so scharpe,
riȝt so me grulde schille harpe.
Þos hule luste þiderward,
& hold hire eȝe noþerwa[r]d,
& sat tosvolle & ibolwe,

The chicks, first one & then another,
all sang out, 'It was our brother,
him whose head sits like a boulder,
shame it's still perched on his shoulders. 120
Fling his foulness to the deck
& where he lands he'll break his neck.'
The falcon's chicks would not tell fibs;
she plucked the stray bird from their midst
& threw it to the forest floor
where crows & magpies gouged & tore.
This fable, though it isn't proof,
delivers an essential truth:
expect no good of any trace
from him born to a lowly race. 130
He might mix with a better class
but can't escape his commonness,
& even in a decent nest
a rotten egg's a rotten egg.
An apple might roll far & wide
& leave its family tree behind,
but at its core it still betrays
its starting place & early days."

Then after hectoring so long
the Nightingale broke out in song, 140
her tune as vibrant & as sharp
as music streaming from a harp.
The Owl took in the songbird's sound,
her eyes fixed firmly on the ground,
& sat there ready to explode,

also ho hadde one frogge isuolȝe:
for ho wel wiste & was iwar
þat ho song hire a-bisemar.
& noþeles ho ȝa[f] andsuare,
"Whi neltu flon into þe bare, 150
& sewi [w]are unker bo
of briȝter howe, of uairur blo?"
"No, þu hauest wel scharpe clawe,
ne kepich noȝt þat þu me clawe.
þu hauest cliuers suþe stronge,
þu tuengst þar-mid so doþ a tonge.
Þu þoȝtest, so doþ þine ilike,
mid faire worde me biswike.
Ich nolde don þat þu me raddest,
ich wiste wel þat þu me misraddest. 160
Schamie þe for þin unrede!
Vnwroȝen is þi svikelhede!
Schild þine svikeldom vram þe liȝte,
& hud þat woȝe amon[g] þe riȝte.
Þane þu wilt þin unriȝt spene,
loke þat hit ne bo isene:
vor svikedom haue[þ] schome & hete,
ȝif hit is ope & underȝete.
Ne speddestu noȝt mid þine unwrenche,
for ich am war & can wel blenche. 170
Ne helpþ noȝt þat þu bo to [þ]riste:
ich wolde viȝte bet mid liste
þan þu mid al þine strengþe.
Ich habbe, on brede & eck on lengþe,
castel god on mine rise:

12

like someone choking on a toad.
She knew full well the other bird
was baiting her with wounding words,
but answered her, "Why don't you show
yourself out here & then we'll know
who wears the fairer face, & who
is finest feathered—me or you."
"No thanks, your talons bite like nails.
I'd rather not become impaled
on sets of claws so hard & strong
they grip their prey like iron tongs.
You mean to snare me with untruth;
that's Owl behavior through & through,
& I'll be paying your advice
no heed because it's laced with lies.
Admit the shame of who you are,
your crooked traits are now laid bare
& so are those deceits you cloak
when spending time with decent folk.
And if you deal in dirty business
check it's done without a witness;
treachery becomes disgrace
when played out in a public place.
Though knowing how to duck & weave
protects me from your evil schemes;
you thrash about, all boast & brawn,
but I do better with my brain
than you with all your thuggish strength,
& on this branch—its breadth & length—
I have my castle. 'He who flies

150

160

170

'Wel fiʒt þat wel fliʒt,' seiþ þe wise.
Ac lete we awei þos cheste,
vor suiche wordes boþ unw[re]ste;
& fo we on mid riʒte dome,
mid faire worde & mid ysome.   *180*
Þeʒ we ne bo at one acorde,
we m[a]ʒe bet mid fayre worde,
witute cheste, & bute fiʒte,
plaidi mid foʒe & mid riʒte:
& mai hure eiþer wat h[e] wile
mid riʒte segge & mid sckile."

Þo quaþ þe hule "[W]u schal us seme,
þat kunne & wille riʒt us deme?"
"Ich wot wel" quaþ þe niʒtingale,
"Ne þaref þarof bo no tale.   *190*
Maister Nichole of Guldeforde,
he is wis an war of worde:
he is of dome suþe gleu,
& him is loþ eurich unþeu.
He wot insiʒt in eche songe,
wo singet wel, wo singet wronge:
& he can schede vrom þe riʒte
þat woʒe, þat þuster from þe liʒte."

Þo hule one wile hi biþoʒte,
& after þan þis word upbroʒte: *200*
"Ich granti wel þat he us deme,
vor þeʒ he were wile breme,
& lof him were niʒtingale,

14

shall win the fight.' So say the wise.
Enough, though, of this bickering,
such barneys are belittling.
Let's start afresh, & this time act
with greater courtesy & tact.
We don't see eye to eye, that's plain,
but both would make a stronger claim
without hostility or spite.
Let's state with dignity & pride
our points, positions & beliefs
in measured tones & reasoned speech."

The Owl replied, "A magistrate
is needed to adjudicate."
"That's easy," said the rossignol,
"his name stands ready on my tongue.   190
The person who should arbitrate
is Master Simon Armitage.
He's skilled with words & worldly wise
& frowns on every form of vice.
In terms of tunes, his ear can tell
who makes a din & who sings well.
He thrives at telling wrong from right
& knows the darkness from the light."

The Owl considered what she'd heard,
then after pondering declared,   200
"Agreed, he'll tell the honest truth,
though he was reckless in his youth
& spooned a Nightingale or two

& oþer wiȝte gente & smale,
ich wot he is nu suþe acoled.
Nis he vor þe noȝt afoled,
þat he, for þine olde luue,
me adun legge & þe buue:
ne schaltu neure so him queme,
þat he for þe fals dom deme.   210
He is him ripe & fast-rede,
ne lust him nu to none unrede:
nu him ne lust na more pleie,
he wile gon a riȝte weie."

Þe niȝtingale was al ȝare,
ho hadde ilorned wel aiware:
"Hule," ho sede, "seie me soþ,
wi dostu þat unwiȝtis doþ?
þu singist aniȝt & noȝt adai,
& al þi song is wailawai.   220
Þu miȝt mid þine songe afere
alle þat ihereþ þine ibere:
þu sch[ri]chest & ȝollest to þine fere,
þat hit is grislich to ihere:
hit þinche[þ] boþe wise & snepe
noȝt þat þu singe, ac þat þu wepe.
Þu fliȝst aniȝt & noȝt adai:
þarof ich w[u]ndri & wel mai.
vor eurich þing þat schuniet riȝt,
hit luueþ þuster & hatiet liȝt: 230
& eurich þing þat is lof misdede,
hit luueþ þuster to his dede.

16

& other passerines like you.
And yet he has cooled down a lot
& doesn't lust for you of late
& wouldn't, through some lingering love,
set me below & you above.
His sense of justice won't be harmed
by your submissions to his heart.   *210*
Mature & of a balanced mind,
all indiscretions left behind,
ignoring every vulgar cause
he steers a straight & proper course."

Schooled in the art of rhetoric
the Nightingale's response was quick.
"So tell me, Owl, why is it true
you do as evil creatures do?
The one nocturnal dirge you sing
is woeful & self-pitying   *220*
& those unlucky souls who hear
are terror-struck with morbid fear.
The squawks you aim toward your mate
disturb the ears they penetrate.
Both dolt & genius have found
your singing makes a weeping sound.
You sleep by day & fly by night,
which worries me, & well it might;
all things preferring wrong to right
adore the dark & hate the light,   *230*
& every sinful creature needs
the night-time to obscure its deeds.

A wis word, þeʒ hit bo unclene,
is fele manne a-muþe imene,
for Alured King hit seide & wrot:
'He schunet þat hine [vu]l wot.'
Ich wene þat þu dost also,
vor þu fliʒst niʒtes euer mo.
An oþer þing me is a-wene,
þu hauest aniʒt wel briʒte sene;   240
bi daie þu art stare-blind,
þat þu ne sichst ne bov ne strind.
Adai þu art blind oþer bisne,
þarbi men segget a uorbisne:
'Riʒt so hit farþ bi þan ungode
þat noʒt ne suþ to none gode,
& is so ful of vuele wrenche
þat him ne mai no man atprenche,
& can wel þane þu[str]e wai,
& þane briʒte lat awai.'   250
So doþ þat boþ of þine cunde,
of liʒte nabbeþ hi none imunde."

Þos hule luste suþe longe,
& was oftoned suþe stronge:
ho quaþ "Þu [h]attest niʒtingale,
þu miʒtest bet hoten galegale,
vor þu hauest to monie tale.
Lat þine tunge habbe spale!
Þu wenest þat þes dai bo þin oʒe:
lat me nu habbe mine þroʒe: 260
bo nu stille & lat me speke,

18

A proverb, vulgar but of note,
(a phrase King Alfred said & wrote)
repeated frequently: 'He slinks
away who knows his own bad stink.'
That summarizes perfectly
your fly-by-night activities.
And something else occurs to me:
in total blackness you can see   *240*
but once the dawn dispels the dark
you struggle telling branch from bark!
And of those beings, who by day
are sightless, this is what they say:
they're ne'er-do-wells & vagabonds
whose shady dealings know no bounds,
whose sneaky schemes & escapades
no decent person can escape,
they tread a shadowed path & shun
the lanes & ways lit by the sun,   *250*
& you're the very same, the type
who lives her life avoiding light."

She listened for what felt an age,
the Owl, then flew into a rage.
"You're called a Nightingale," she spat,
"but blabbermouth's more accurate.
Your monologues are all-consuming,
rest your tongue & stop assuming
that you've won the day & own
the argument. Give me my turn   *260*
& keep your trap shut while I speak

ich wille bon of þe awreke.
& lust hu ich con me bitelle,
mid riȝte soþe, witute spelle.
Þu seist þat ich me hude adai,
þarto ne segge ich nich ne nai:
& lust ich telle þe wareuore,
al wi hit is & wareuore.
Ich habbe bile stif & stronge,
& gode cliuers scharp & longe,   *270*
so hit bicumeþ to hauekes cunne;
hit is min hiȝte, hit is mi w[u]nne,
þat ich me draȝe to mine cunde,
ne mai [me] no man þareuore schende:
on me hit is wel isene,
vor riȝte cunde ich am so kene.
Vorþi ich am loþ smale foȝle
þat floþ bi grunde an bi þuuele:
hi me bichermet & bigredeþ,
& hore flockes to [m]e ledeþ.   *280*
Me is lof to habbe reste
& sitte stille in mine neste:
vor nere ich neuer no þe betere,
[ȝ]if ich mid chauling & mid chatere
hom schende & mid fule worde,
so herdes doþ oþer mid schit-worde.
Ne lust me wit þe screwen chide;
forþi ich wende from hom wide.
Hit is a wise monne dome,
& hi hit segget wel ilome,   *290*
þat me ne chide wit þe gidie,

20

& listen closely while I seek
a rational & sincere revenge
without recourse to verbiage.
You say by day I hibernate,
a fact I won't repudiate,
but hear me while I clarify
the wherefore & the reasons why.
My beak is powerful & strong,
my claws are sharp & very long,   *270*
& rightfully I share these traits
with others of the owlish trade.
No man can criticize my pride
in feeling kinship with my tribe.
Look at my features & you'll find
ferocity personified,
so all the tiny birds abhor me,
flitting through the understory,
slighting me with squeaks & squawks
& flying at me in their flocks   *280*
when all I want to do is rest
in peaceful silence on my nest.
I'll fare no better if I shriek
& curse my enemies, or speak
the kind of oaths & foul abuse
& filthy talk that shepherds use.
Instead of wasting words with knaves
I'd rather look the other way.
The wise have noted more than once
that he who argues with a dunce   *290*
might just as well compare his jaw

ne wit þan ofne me ne ȝonie.
At sume siþe herde [I] telle
hu Alured sede on his spelle:
'Loke þat þu ne bo þare
þar chauling boþ & cheste ȝare:
lat sottes chide & uorþ þu go.'
& ich am wis & do also.
& ȝet Alured seide an oþer side
a word þat is isprunge wide: 300
'Þat wit þe fule haueþ imene,
ne cumeþ he neuer from him cleine.'
Wenestu þat haueck bo þe worse
þoȝ crowe bigrede him bi þe mershe,
& goþ to him mid hore chirme
riȝt so hi wille wit him schirme?
Þe hauec folȝeþ gode rede,
& fliȝt his wei & lat him grede."
"Ȝet þu me seist of oþer þinge,
& telst þat ich ne can noȝt singe,   310
ac al mi rorde is woning,
& to ihire grislich þing.
Þat nis noȝt soþ, ich singe efne,
mid fulle dreme & lude stefne.
Þu wenist þat ech song bo grislich,
þat þine pipinge nis ilich.
Mi stefne is [bold] & noȝt unorne,
ho is ilich one grete horne,
& þin is ilich one pipe,
of one smale wode unripe.   320
Ich singe bet þan þu dest:

22

against an oven's yawning door.
And now a saying comes to mind,
a proverb that King Alfred coined:
'Be careful not to waste your life
where strife & quarreling are rife;
keep well away from fractious fools.'
A wise Owl, I obey those rules.
A further point that Alfred makes
is quoted far & wide. It states: 300
'Those mixing with a filthy kind
shall never leave the dirt behind.'
Therefore, a hawk is none the worse
if crows along the marsh rehearse
their jeers & jibes, then swoop & squawk
as if they mean to fell the hawk.
The hawk, though, follows sound advice:
he lets them shriek, then off he flies.
And there's a further charge you bring,
the accusation I can't sing,   310
& that my song is one long moan,
a painful, monotonal drone.
It isn't so. My voice, being true,
emits a rich, melodious tune.
You twitter, so for you a song
that doesn't cheep & chirp is wrong.
My call is deep & bold & proud
& booms out with a horn-like sound,
while yours pipes like a tinny reed
sliced from a thin unripened weed.   320
My song is best, yours pleases least,

23

þu chaterest so doþ on Irish prost.
Ich singe an eue a riʒte time,
& soþþe won hit is bed-time,
þe þridde siþe a[t] middel-niʒte:
& so ich mine song adiʒte
wone ich iso arise vorre
oþer dai-rim oþer dai-sterre.
Ich do god mid mine þrote,
& warni men to hore note.   330
Ac þu singest alle longe niʒt,
from eue fort hit is dai-liʒt,
& eure seist þin o song
so longe so þe niʒt is long:
& eure croweþ þi wrecche crei,
þat he ne swikeþ niʒt ne dai.
Mid þine pipinge þu adunest
þas monnes earen þar þu wunest,
& makest þine song so unw[u]rþ
þa[t] me ne telþ of þar noʒ[t] w[u]rþ.   340
Eurich murʒþe mai so longe ileste
þat ho shal liki wel unwreste:
vor harpe, & pipe, & fuʒeles [song]
mislikeþ, ʒif hit is to long.
Ne bo þe song neuer so murie,
þat he ne shal þinche wel unmurie
ʒef he ilesteþ ouer unwille:
so þu miʒt þine song aspille.
Vor hit is soþ, Alured hit seide,
& me hit mai ine boke rede: 350
'Eurich þing mai losen his godhede

24

you witter like an Irish priest!
I sing at dusk—the proper hour—
& then at bedtime sing once more,
then sing again when midnight chimes;
my songs are governed by those times.
I see the distant dawn draw near
& watch the morning star appear
then from my throat a note is shaped
that summons workers to their trade.   330
But you sing all & every night
from sunset through to morning light,
the whole night long you sing a song
that prattles on & on & on,
an exhibitionist display
that chirps away throughout the day
& causes trauma in the ears
of anybody living near,
a song so cheap it has no worth
for people anywhere on earth.   340
For as a rule, a thing that pleases
rankles if it never ceases;
harps & pipes & songs of birds
eventually disturb the nerves,
just as the cheeriest of scores
seems not so cheery any more
if endlessly performed. Your song
is likewise wastefully prolonged.
A noble stance that Alfred took
(it's written down in many books):   350
'When overdone, true virtue fades.

25

mid unmeþe & mid ouerdede.'
Mid este þu þe miȝt ouerquatie,
& ouerfulle makeþ wlatie:
an eurich mureȝþe mai agon
ȝif me hit halt eure forþ in on,
bute one, þat is Godes riche,
þat eure is svete & eure iliche:
þeȝ þu nime eure o[f] þan lepe,
hit is eure ful bi hepe.   *360*
Wunder hit is of Godes riche,
þat eure spenþ & euer is iliche.

ȝut þu me seist an oþer shome,
þat ich a[m] on mine eȝen lome,
an seist, for þat ich flo bi niȝte,
þat ich ne mai iso bi liȝte.
Þu liest! on me hit is isene
þat ich habbe gode sene:
vor nis non so dim þusternesse
þat ich euer iso þe lasse.   *370*
Þu wenest þat ich ne miȝte iso,
vor ich bi daie noȝt ne flo.
Þe hare luteþ al dai,
ac noþeles iso he mai.
ȝif hundes urneþ to him-ward,
[h]e gengþ wel suiþe awai-ward,
& hokeþ paþes suiþe narewe,
& haueþ mid him his blenches ȝarewe,
& hupþ & star[t] suþe coue,
an secheþ paþes to þe groue: *380*

26

With overkill, real value wanes.
Indulgence, surplus & excess
do not equate to more, but less,
& what goes on relentlessly
infuriates eventually.'
The only everlasting good
is found within the realm of God:
its basket constantly provides
yet stays replenished to all sides.   *360*
God's wondrous empire knows no end,
forever giving, never spent.

"A further slander: you have dared
to say my vision is impaired,
assuming that I fly by night
because I'm blinded by the light.
But clearly you are telling lies;
I know that I have perfect eyes
since there's no dim or darkened state
my piercing gaze can't penetrate.   *370*
I have defective sight, you say,
because I never fly by day,
but skulking through those hours, the hare
is master of the watchful stare.
Flushed from his form by hunting hounds
at breakneck pace away he bounds
down steep & curved & narrow tracks,
all twists & turns & clever tricks,
until with leaps & darts he speeds
toward the cover of the trees.   *380*

ne sholde he uor boþe his eȝe
so don, ȝif he þe bet niseȝe.
Ich mai ison so wel so on hare,
þeȝ ich bi daie sitte an dare.
Þar aȝte men [boþ] in worre,
an fareþ boþe ner an forre,
an oueruareþ fele [þ]ode,
an doþ bi niȝte gode node,
ich folȝi þan aȝte manne,
an flo bi niȝte in hore banne."

Þe niȝtingale in hire þoȝte
athold al þis, & longe þoȝte
wat ho þarafter miȝte segge:
vor ho ne miȝte noȝt alegge
þat þe hule hadde hire ised,
vor he spac boþe riȝt an red.
An hire ofþuȝte þat ho hadde
þe speche so for uorþ iladde,
an was oferd þat hire answare
ne w[u]rþe noȝt ariȝt ifare.

Ac noþeles he spac boldeliche,
vor he is wis þat hardeliche
wiþ is uo berþ grete ilete,
þat he uor areȝþe hit ne forlete:
vor suich worþ bold ȝif þu [fliȝst],
þat w[u]lle flo ȝif þu [n]isvicst;
ȝif he isiþ þat þu nart areȝ,
he wile of [bore] w[u]rchen bareȝ.

Coordination of that kind
is not accomplished by the blind!
I hide away by day but share
outstanding eyesight with the hare.
When fearless soldiers march to war,
advancing on all fronts, the corps
engaging evil foreign powers
& fighting through the darkest hours,
I keep them company, my flight
a flag above them in the night."   390

Left to her thoughts, the Nightingale
then mulled things over for a while,
not confident she could deny
the soundness of the Owl's reply,
because with that robust defense
the Owl had spoken truth & sense.
Perhaps her judgment had been wrong
to let the rumpus last this long,
& now it was her turn to speak
her logic might sound false or weak.   400
But she was bold & held her nerve,
&, wisely, spoke with guts & verve,
& looked her foe straight in the face.
The timid voice will lose the case;
a rival prospers if he sees
you run—stand firm though & he flees,
or met by fortitude he'll flip
from fierce wild boar to gelded pig.

29

& forþi, þeȝ þe niȝtingale
were aferd, ho spac bolde tale.   410

"[H]ule" ho seide "wi dostu so?
þu singest a-winter wolawo!
þu singest so doþ hen a-snowe,
al þat ho singeþ hit is for wowe.
A-wintere þu singest wroþe & ȝomere,
an eure þu art dumb a-sumere.
Hit is for þine fule niþe
þat þu ne miȝt mid us bo bliþe,
vor þu forbernest wel neȝ for onde
wane ure blisse cumeþ to londe.   420
þu farest so doþ þe ille,
evrich blisse him is unwille:
grucching & luring him boþ rade,
ȝif he isoþ þat men boþ glade.
He wolde þat he iseȝe
teres in evrich monnes eȝe:
ne roȝte he þeȝ flockes were
imeind bi toppes & bi here.
Al so þu dost on þire side:
vor wanne snov liþ þicke & wide,   430
an alle wiȝtes habbeþ sorȝe,
þu singest from eue fort a-morȝe.
Ac ich alle blisse mid me bringe:
ech wiȝt is glad for mine þinge,
& blisseþ hit wanne ich cume,
& hiȝteþ aȝen mine kume.
Þe blostme ginneþ springe & sprede,

30

And so, despite all doubts & fears,
the Nightingale was loud & clear.

She answered, "Owl, why do you croon
a miserable & gloomy tune
each winter? Like a hen in snow
complaining of its grief & woe
you gripe & groan all season long,
then come the summer you play dumb!
Pure malice means that you can't bear
the happiness that others share,
& your resentments fume & burn
wherever pleasure takes its turn.
You're like some old curmudgeon, riled
by every laugh or blissful smile,
a true-born killjoy fueled by spite
who hates a sweet or cheerful sight.
You smirk & simper when you hear
of men whose faces stream with tears.
When wool gets tangled up with hair
the weaver weeps & you don't care.
That's where you stand—on sorrow's side—
so when the snow lies deep & wide
with every bird & beast forlorn,
you drone your dirge from dusk to dawn.
But gladness spreads when I arrive
to every animal alive;
folk eagerly anticipate
my coming, which they celebrate!
Then flowers bloom & branches bud

boþe ine tro & ek on mede.
Þe lilie mid hire faire wlite
wolcumeþ me, þat þu hit w[i]te,   440
bit me mid hire faire blo
þat ich shulle to hire flo.
Þe rose also mid hire rude,
þat cumeþ ut of þe þorne wode,
bit me þat ich shulle singe
vor hire luue one skentinge:
& ich so do þurȝ niȝt & dai,
þe more ich singe þe more I mai,
an skente hi mid mine songe,
ac noþeles noȝt ouerlonge;   450
wane ich iso þat men boþ glade,
ich nelle þat hi bon to sade:
þan is ido vor wan ich com,
ich fare aȝen & do wisdom.
Wane mon hoȝeþ of his sheue,
an falewi cumeþ on grene leue,
ich fare hom & nime leue:
ne recche ich noȝt of winteres reue.
wan ich iso þat cumeþ þat harde,
ich fare hom to min erde,   460
an habbe boþe luue & þonc
þat ich her com & hider swonk.
Þan min erende is ido,
sholde ich bileue? nai, [w]arto?
vor he nis noþer ȝep ne wis,
þat longe abid þar him nod nis."

across the fields & through the wood.
The lily's luminescent glow
beams out & greets me, as you know,   *440*
her countenance—so bright & fair—
inviting me to fly to her.
The rose as well, her face of fire
emerging from a thorny briar,
imploring me to stir & sing
her praises with some loving hymn.
I sing both night & day, therefore,
& if it pleases I sing more,
enchanting people with my song
though careful not to sing too long,   *450*
for when I witness happy men
I know to stop indulging them;
once my performance is complete
I choose to make a wise retreat.
When men attend their ripened sheaves
& greenness withers from the leaves,
that's when I turn & take my leave,
migrating far from winter's reach;
I see the weather turning &
I head off to my native land,   *460*
but not before I'm thanked & loved
for toiling in this neighborhood.
Yes, once the task is carried out
I'm gone! Why would I hang about?
It's neither prudent nor inspired
to linger longer than required."

Þos hule luste, & leide an hord
al þis mot, word after word,
an after þoȝte hu he miȝte
ansvere uinde best mid riȝte: 470
vor he mot hine ful wel biþenche,
þat is aferd of plaites wrenche.

"Þv aishest me," þe hule sede,
"wi ich a-winter singe & grede.
Hit is gode monne iwone,
an was from þe worlde frome,
þat ech god man his frond icnowe,
an blisse mid hom sume þrowe
in his huse at his borde,
mid faire speche & faire worde.   480
& hure & hure to Cristesmasse,
þane riche & poure, more & lasse,
singeþ cundut niȝt & dai,
ich hom helpe what ich mai.
& ek ich þenche of oþer þinge
þane to pleien oþer to singe.
Ich habbe herto gode ansuare
anon iredi & al ȝare:
vor sumeres-tide is al to [w]lonc,
an doþ misreken monnes þonk: 490
vor he ne recþ noȝt of clennesse,
al his þoȝt is of golnesse:
vor none dor no leng nabideþ,
ac eurich upon oþer rideþ:
þe sulue stottes ine þe stode

The Owl considered what she'd heard,
digested each & every word
& pondered how she might redress
such comments in her next address,   *470*
for those aware of verbal tricks
must cautiously assess the risks.

The Owl replied, "You ask me why
all winter through I call & cry.
Well, it's a common trait of man
& has been since the world began
that worthy friends will congregate
with worthy friends to celebrate;
at table, in the home, good folk
exchanging mirth & pleasant talk,   *480*
particularly at Christmas time
when rich & poor & low & high
will sing their carols night & day.
I like to help them when I may,
but my concerns & cares belong
to deeper things than games & song,
to wit, I have a smart response
which I'll communicate at once.
In summer, heady feelings reign
that meddle with a fellow's brain   *490*
& turn his pure, unsullied mind
to notions of a lustful kind,
& not one living thing can wait
to mount his mate & copulate,
& frisky stallions in the stud

boþ boþe wilde & mere-wode.
& þu sulf art þar-among,
for of golnesse is al þi song,
an aȝen þet þu w[i]lt teme,
þu art wel modi & wel breme.   *500*
Sone so þu hau[e]st itrede,
ne miȝtu leng a word iqueþe,
ac pipest al so doþ a mose,
mid chokeringe, mid steune hose.
ȝet þu singst worse þon þe heisugge,
[þ]at fliȝþ bi grunde among þe stubbe:
wane þi lust is ago,
þonne is þi song ago also.
A-sumere chorles awedeþ
& uorcrempeþ & uorbredeþ: *510*
hit nis for luue noþeles,
ac is þe chorles wode res;
vor wane he haueþ ido his dede,
ifallen is al his boldhede,
habbe he istunge under gore,
ne last his luue no leng more.
Al so hit is on þine mode:
so sone so þu sittest a-brode,
þu forlost al þine wise.
Al so þu farest on þine rise: *520*
wane þu hauest ido þi gome,
þi steune goþ anon to shome.
Ac [w]ane niȝtes cumeþ longe,
& b[r]ingeþ forstes starke an stronge,
þanne erest hit is isene

would ride each filly if they could.
And you're the center of the throng
with your debauched, licentious song.
So when it's time to do the deed
you brag about your need to breed,   500
but once your wanton act is done
you're spent, & suddenly struck dumb,
or cackle with a blue tit's voice
& make a cracked & croaky noise.
In fact, your song's worse than a sparrow's,
grubbing through the stubbled furrows;
once desire has run its course
your throat dries up & leaves you hoarse.
Throughout the summer months, the yokels
writhe & wriggle, but those locals   510
aren't possessed by love—their limbs & loins
are at the mercy of their groins.
And when his primal urge has passed
a man's great ardor will collapse;
he worms his way inside a skirt
then falls down lifeless & inert.
It's very similar with your mood:
the day you nestle on your brood
your song comes to a sudden stop
& on your perch your bolt is shot;   520
once all the thrills & spills are done
it leaves you with a slackened tongue.
But when the nights turn long & dark
& bitter frost lies deep & sharp
then soon enough it's obvious

war is þe snelle, [w]ar is þe kene.
At þan harde me mai auinde
[w]o geþ forþ, wo liþ bihinde.
Me mai ison at þare node,
[w]an me shal harde wike bode;   *530*
þanne ich am snel & pleie & singe,
& hiзte me mid mi skentinge:
of none wintere ich ne recche,
vor ich nam non asv[u]nde wrecche.
& ek ich frouri uele wiзte
þat mid hom nabbe[þ] none miзtte:
hi boþ hoзfule & uel arme,
an secheþ зorne to þe warme;
oft ich singe uor hom þe more
for lutli sum of hore sore.   *540*
Hu þincþ þe? artu зut inume?
Artu mid riзte ouercume?"

"Nay, nay!" sede þe niзtingale,
"þu shalt ihere anoþer tale:
зet nis þos speche ibroзt to dome.
Ac bo wel stille, & lust nu to me
ich shal mid one bare worde
do þat þi speche [wurþ] forworþe."

"Þat nere noht riзt" þe hule sede,
"þu hauest bicloped al so þu bede,   *550*
an ich þe habbe iзiue ansuare.
Ac ar we to unker dome fare,
ich wille speke toward þe

38

who's resolute & vigorous.
It's during hardship that we find
who goes ahead, who lags behind,
& who amongst us doesn't shirk
when delegated to the work.   530
That's when I'm at my liveliest
& singing at my blissful best.
In winter months, I'm never vexed
because I'm not some feeble wretch.
I comfort creatures that are known
to have no courage of their own,
the apprehensive & forlorn
who long for somewhere safe & warm.
I often sing them my refrain
as consolation for their pain.   540
At which point shall I rest my case?
Are you out-thought? Put in your place?"

The Nightingale said, "No. Now listen
closely to my next submission.
There's no verdict on this bout
as yet. Be calm & hear me out,
I'll win it with a single move
which no appealing will disprove."

"That isn't fair," the Owl complained,
"As promised you have made your claims   550
which I have answered, as you know.
Before we seek a judgment, though,
I mean to score a point or two

al so þu speke toward me;
an þu me ansuare ȝif þu miȝt.
Seie me nu, þu wrecche wiȝt,
is in þe eni oþer note
bute þu hauest schille þrote?
Þu nart noȝt to non oþer þinge,
bute þu canst of chateringe: 560
vor þu art lutel an unstrong,
an nis þi regel noþing long.
Wat dostu godes among monne?
Na mo þe deþ a w[re]cche wranne.
Of þe ne cumeþ non oþer god,
bute þu gredest suich þu bo wod:
an bo þi piping ouergo,
ne boþ on þe craftes namo.
Alured sede, þat was wis:
(he miȝte wel, for soþ hit is,)   570
'Nis no man for is bare songe
lof ne w[u]rþ noȝt suþe longe:
vor þat is a forworþe man
þat bute singe noȝt ne can.'
Þu nart bute on forworþe þing:
on þe nis bute chatering.
Þu art dim an of fule howe,
an þinchest a lutel soti clowe.
Þu nart fair, no þu nart strong,
ne þu nart þicke, ne þu nart long: 580
þu hauest imist al of fairhede,
an lutel is al þi godede.
An oþer þing of þe ich mene,

& speak as I've been spoken to,
so if you're able, do reply.
You sorry creature, please describe
what other purpose you fulfill
apart from being very shrill!
Your only talent as a critter
seems to be your endless witter,   *560*
& you're puny & you sport
a mantle that's unseemly short.
You're no more use to other men
than the pathetic little wren,
& what advancement ever came
from those whose singing sounds insane?
Plus, once your song has petered out
you've nothing else to brag about.
Wise Alfred said—& well he might
since it is absolutely right—   *570*
that none are loved for very long
just for their aptitude for song,
& it's a useless, worthless thing
that can't do any more than sing.
You're empty but for chirping chatter,
nothing else about you matters.
And you're dirty, drab, & look
no better than a ball of soot.
You lack all prettiness & strength
& come up short in height & length.   *580*
If Beauty called, it didn't stay,
& Virtue looked the other way.
Another charge that I will file:

þu nart vair ne þu nart clene.
Wane þu comest to manne haȝe,
þar þornes boþ & ris idraȝe,
bi hegge & bi þicke wode,
þar men goþ oft to hore node,
þarto þu draȝst, þarto þu w[u]nest,
an oþer clene stede þu schunest. 590
Þan ich flo niȝtes after muse,
I mai þe uinde ate rum-huse;
among þe wode, among þe netle,
þu sittest & singst bihinde þe setle:
þar me mai þe ilomest finde,
þar men worpeþ hore bihinde.
Ȝet þu atuitest me mine mete,
an seist þat ich fule wiȝtes ete.
Ac wat etestu, þat þu ne liȝe,
bute attercoppe & fule ulige, 600
an wormes, ȝif þu miȝte finde
among þe uolde of harde rinde?
Ȝet ich can do wel gode wike,
vor ich can loki manne wike:
an mine wike boþ wel gode,
vor ich helpe to manne uode.
Ich can nimen mus at berne,
an ek at chirche ine þe derne:
vor me is lof to Cristes huse,
to clansi hit wiþ fule muse, 610
ne schal þar neure come to
ful wiȝt, ȝif ich hit mai iuo.
An ȝif me lust one mi skentinge

your habits, like your looks, are vile.
Arriving at a person's plot
where thorns & branches knit & knot
by hedgerows & by tangled weeds
where people go to squat & pee,
that's where you like to hang around
& won't withdraw to cleaner ground.   590
At night, while I pursue the mouse
you loiter by that smelly house
perched on a nettle or a reed,
at song behind the toilet seat.
It's there you frequently appear,
where people bend & bare their rear.
Disdainfully you say I eat
all kinds of squalid insect meat,
yet hypocritically you lunch
on horrid flies & spiders, munch   600
through worms & creepy-crawly bugs
found in the tree bark where you grub.
I undertake essential tasks
where people live, performing acts
that folk find helpful, doing good
where humans house their stock of food.
I prey on vermin dusk to dawn
both in the church & in the barn.
It is my pleasure in Christ's house
to hunt down every filthy mouse;   610
no rodent will live safely there
while I patrol it from the air.
Alternatively, I might choose

to wernen oþer w[u]nienge,
ich habbe at wude tron wel grete,
mit þicke boȝe noþing blete,
mid iui grene al bigrowe,
þat eure stont iliche iblowe,
an his hou neuer ne uorlost,
wan hit sniuw ne wan hit frost.   620
Þarin ich habbe god ihold,
a-winter warm, a-sumere cold.
Wane min hus stont briȝt & grene,
of þine nis noþing isene.
Ȝet þu me telst of oþer þinge,
of mine briddes seist gabbinge,
þat hore nest nis noȝt clene.
Hit is fale oþer wiȝte imene:
vor hors a-stable & oxe a-stalle
[d]oþ al þat hom wule þar falle.   630
An lutle children in þe cradele,
boþe chorles an ek aþele,
[d]oþ al þat in hore ȝoeþe
þat hi uorleteþ in hore duȝeþe.
Wat! can þat ȝongling hit bihede?
Ȝif hit misdeþ, hit mo[t] nede:
a uorbisne is of olde i[vu]rne,
[þ]at node makeþ old wif urne.
An ȝet ich habbe an oþer andsware:
wiltu to mine neste uare   640
an loki hu hit is idiȝt?
Ȝif þu art wis lorni þu [miȝt]:
mi nest is holȝ & rum amidde,

44

some different dwelling for my roost:
great trees stand in the wood, & there
the sturdy boughs are never bare
but overgrown with ivy vines
whose leafy tendrils intertwine,
whose verdant tones are never lost
through any weather, snow or frost.   620
My stronghold in those trunks & arms—
in summer cool, in winter warm—
is always green & always bright
when yours has disappeared from sight.
Another groundless charge you lay
insults my little chicks. You say
their nest is sullied by their feces—
this is true of many species:
stabled horses, oxen in their stalls,
all leave their droppings where they fall,   630
& infant children in their cots,
of lowly birth, of courtly stock,
do certain things when newly born
they cease to do when fully grown.
To blame the fledgling is unjust;
it toilets when & where it must.
An ancient proverb wisely states:
'The crone will sprint if need dictates.'
A further issue: I suggest
you come with me & see my nest.   640
By noting how it's organized
you'll be enlightened—if you're wise.
Within a wide & hollow space

45

so hit is softest mine bridde.
Hit is broiden al abute,
vrom þe neste uor wiþute:
þarto hi go[þ] to hore node,
ac þat þu menest ich hom forbode.
We nimeþ ȝeme of manne bure,
an after þan we makeþ ure: 650
men habbet, among oþer i[h]ende,
a rum-hus at hore bures ende,
vor þat hi nelleþ to uor go,
an mine briddes doþ al so.
Site nu stille, chaterestre!
nere þu neuer ibunde uastre:
herto ne uindestu neuer andsware.
Hong up þin ax! nu þu miȝt fare!"

Þe niȝtingale at þisse worde
was wel neȝ ut of rede iworþe,   660
an þoȝte ȝorne on hire mode
ȝif ho oȝt elles understode,
ȝif ho kuþe oȝt bute singe,
þat miȝte helpe to oþer þinge.
Herto ho moste andswere uinde,
oþer mid alle bon bihinde:
an hit is suþe strong to fiȝte
aȝen soþ & aȝen riȝte.
He mot gon to al mid ginne,
þan þe horte boþ on [w]inne: 670
an þe man mot on oþer segge,

my fledglings have their bedding place,
but interlocked around the edge
the criss-crossed lattice forms a ledge
& there my youngsters void their bowels.
What practice you suggest, we owls
forbid. We watch man build his home
then in its image build our own.   *650*
All human beings build their loos
close to their homes and we do too.
They value such convenience—
we want the same experience!
Now stop your chelping, chatterbox,
you've never been so tied in knots.
To my remarks you've no riposte;
hang up your axe, your case is lost."

Those comments stunned the Nightingale;
she tried to answer back, but failed.   *660*
She racked her brains, at pains to find
a clear example in her mind
that proved her usefulness, one thing
that she could do apart from sing,
& had to squash the other's claim
or lose advantage in the game,
though it's not easy to rebut
contentions that are so well put.
The man whose self-assurance slips
must turn to scheming & to wit   *670*
& use the language of disguise.

he mot bihemmen & bilegge,
ȝif muþ wiþute mai biwro
þat me þe horte noȝt niso:
an sone mai a word misreke
þar muþ shal aȝen horte speke;
an sone mai a word misstorte
þar muþ shal speken aȝen horte.
Ac noþeles ȝut upe þon,
her is to red wo hine kon: *680*
vor neuer nis wit so kene
so þane red him is a-wene.
þanne erest kume[þ] his ȝephede
wone hit is alre-mest on drede:
for Aluered seide of olde quide,
an ȝut hit nis of horte islide:
"Wone þe bale is alre-hecst,
þonne is þe bote alre-necst";
vor wit west among his sore,
an for his sore hit is þe more.   *690*
Vorþi nis neuere mon redles
ar his horte bo witles:
ac ȝif þat he forlost his wit,
þonne is his red-purs al to-slit;
ȝif he ne kon his wit atholde,
ne uint he red in one uolde.
Vor Alur[e]d seide, þat wel kuþe,
eure he spac mid soþe muþe:
"Wone þe bale is alre-hecst,
þanne is þe bote alre-nest."   *700*

48

When talking he should improvise
so that his mouth does not reveal
the feelings that his mind conceals,
and arguments will fall apart
when out of kilter with the heart
& words depart from their design
when heart & tongue are misaligned.
Any yet, by means well known to some,
such obstacles are overcome: 680
the brain is at its cunning best
when challenged by a crucial test,
& when a prize is most at risk
the mind devises crafty tricks.
As Alfred's ancient proverb tells
(an adage we remember well):
"Not till the worst predicament
is resolution imminent."
For guile not only comes alive
at crisis point, it truly thrives,   690
so no man is a helpless cause
while artfulness directs his course,
but if his bag of tricks should split
inventive thoughts slip through the slit,
& once resourcefulness departs
all schemes & tactics fall apart.
As Alfred said both well & true
(& Alfred knew a thing or two):
"When out & out disaster looms
a remedy will follow soon."   700

Þe niʒtingale al hire hoʒe
mid rede hadde wel bitoʒe;
among þe harde, among þe toʒte,
ful wel mid rede hire biþoʒte,
an hadde andsuere gode ifunde
among al hire harde stunde.

"[H]ule, þu axest me," ho seide,
"ʒif ich kon eni oþer dede
bute singen in sume tide,
an bringe blisse for & wide.   710
Wi axestu of craftes mine?
Betere is min on þan alle þine,
betere is o song of mine muþe
þan al þat eure þi kun kuþe:
an lust, ich telle þe wareuore.
Wostu to wan man was ibore?
To þare blisse of houene-riche,
þar euer is song & murʒþe iliche:
þider fundeþ eurich man
þat eni þing of gode kan.   720
Vorþi me singþ in holi-chirche,
an clerkes ginneþ songes wirche,
þat man iþenche bi þe songe
wider he shal, & þar bon longe:
þat he þe murʒþe ne uorʒete,
ac þarof þenche & biʒete,
an nime ʒeme of chirche steuene,
hu murie is þe blisse of houene.
Clerkes, munekes, & kanunes,

50

Therefore, the Nightingale, though pressed,
stood poised to do her very best,
because the stresses & the strains
had urged the bird to rack her brains
& stage the kind of argument
required by her predicament.

The Nightingale said, "Owl, you ask
why I pursue no other task
than singing out my summer airs
& spreading pleasure everywhere.   *710*
And yet my single art transcends
the whole of your accomplishments:
one song of mine has greater worth
than all the Owl songs on this earth.
Now listen to me & you'll learn
why man was born: it was to yearn
for all the bliss in heaven's domain
where joyful singing never wanes,
toward which, those of virtue strive
as best they can throughout their lives.   *720*
That's why there's singing in the kirks
& holy clerks perform their works,
so man will know by means of song
where he is bound & will belong,
& rather than forget the bliss
will ponder it & make it his,
& understand from hearing hymns
what great rejoicing heaven brings.
All canons, monks & clerks, at home

þar boþ þos gode wicke-tunes,   730
ariseþ up to midel-niȝte,
an singeþ of þe houene-liȝte:
an prostes upe londe singeþ,
wane þe liȝt of daie springeþ.
An ich hom helpe wat I mai,
ich singe mid hom niȝt & dai,
an ho boþ alle for me þe gladdere,
an to þe songe boþ þe raddere.
Ich warni men to hore gode,
þat hi bon bliþe on hore mode,   740
an bidde þat hi moten iseche
þan ilke song þat euer is eche.
Nu þu miȝt, hule, sitte & clinge:
her-among nis no chateringe:
ich graunti þat [w]e go to dome
tofore þe [sulfe Pope] of Rome.
Ac abid ȝete, noþeles,
þu shalt ihere an oþer [h]es;
ne shaltu, for Engelonde,
at þisse worde me atstonde.   750
Wi atuitestu me mine unstrengþe,
an mine ungrete & mine unlengþe,
an seist þat ich nam noȝt strong,
vor ich nam noþer gret ne long?
Ac þu nost neuer wat þu menst,
bute lese wordes þu me lenst:
for ich kan craft & ich kan liste,
an [þ]areuore ich am þus þriste.
Ich kan wit & song man[t]eine,

52

in good communities, are known
to rise from sleep when midnight strikes
& sing in praise of heaven's light,
& priests from country parishes
will sing as night-time vanishes,
& I assist as best I can
by singing day & night to man,
&, heartened by my trilling, he
sings out himself more willingly.
All prudent people, I announce,
should keep a cheerful countenance,
& strive to hear their whole life long
the sound of that eternal song.
And so, Owl, you can sit & rot,
because such feuding fails, & what
we cannot settle on our own
should go before the Pope in Rome.
However, wait a while, for there
are other matters to be aired,
& telling words you won't escape
if England's future were at stake!
Why do you say I'm understrength
& small in size & short in length,
& why insist that I'm not strong
because I'm neither tall nor long?
You are deluded in your aims
to smear me with deceitful claims,
for I'm ingenious & shrewd
& not a little self-assured,
well-versed in song & many sorts

ne triste ich to non oþer maine:
vor soþ hit is þat seide Alured:
'Ne mai no strengþe aʒen red.'
Oft spet wel a lute liste,
þar muche strengþe sholde miste;
mid lutle strengþe, þurʒ ginne,
castel & burʒ me mai iwinne.
Mid liste me mai walle[s] felle,
an worpe of horsse kniʒtes snelle.
Vuel strengþe is lutel wurþ,*

  * * * * *

   * * * * *

ac wisdom naueþ non euening.
An hors is strengur þan a mon;
ac for hit non iwit ne kon,
hit berþ on rugge grete semes,
an draʒþ biuore grete temes,
an þoleþ boþe ʒerd & spure,
an stont iteid at mulne dure.
An hit deþ þat mon hit hot:
an for þan þat hit no wit not,
ne mai his strenþe hit ishilde
þat hit nabuʒþ þe lutle childe.
Mon deþ, mid strengþe & mid witte,
þat oþer þing nis non his fitte.

* Lines 770 and 771 are missing from the Cotton manuscript, but are
easily reclaimed from the Jesus manuscript, and read as follows:
770 Ac wisdom ne w[u]rþ neuer vnw[u]rþ:
771 þu myth iseo þurh alle þing,

of tricks—I don't rely on force.   760
Because it's true what Alfred said:
'The fist is conquered by the head.'
A streak of canniness prevails
where means of might & muscle fail,
& towns & citadels will fall
with very little force at all,
since guile makes walls come crashing down,
throws knights on horseback to the ground.
Raw strength is worthless, but the brain
will triumph time & time again;   770
look where you please, it's evident
good sense has no equivalent.
A man is weaker than a horse
but lacking nous a horse is forced
to bear great burdens on its back
& feel the strain of plow & tack,
withstand the spur & whip, endure
being tethered by the millhouse door,
& through its ignorance must do
exactly what man tells it to,   780
&, strong as it might be, obey
what even tiny children say.
Though man has strength, it is his mind
that leaves all creatures far behind;

Þeȝ alle strengþe at one were,
monnes wit ȝet more were;
vor þe mon mid his crafte,
ouerkumeþ al orþliche shafte.
Al so ich do mid mine one songe
bet þan þu al þe ȝer longe: 790
vor mine crafte men me luuieþ,
vor þine strengþe men þe shunieþ.
Telstu bi me þe wurs for þan
þat ich bute anne craft ne kan?
Ȝif tueie men goþ to wraslinge,
an eiþer oþer faste þringe,
an þe on can swenges suþe fele,
an kan his wrenches wel forhele,
an þe oþer ne can sweng but anne,
an þe is god wiþ eche manne,   800
an mid þon one leiþ to grunde
anne after oþer a lutle stunde,
[w]at þarf he recche of a mo swenge,
þone þe on him is swo genge?
Þ[u] seist þat þu canst fele wike,
ac euer ich am þin unilike.
Do þine craftes alle togadere,
ȝet is min on horte betere.
Oft þan hundes foxes driueþ,
þe kat ful wel him sulue liueþ,   810
þeȝ he ne kunne wrench bute anne.
Þe fo[x] so godne ne can nanne,
þe[ȝ] he kunne so uele wrenche,
þat he wenþ eche hunde atprenche.

56

collective vigor never can
stand equal to the wit of man,
& so through intellect man shall
rule over every animal.
I manage more with just one song
than you achieve the whole year long.   *790*
For my great talent I am loved,
for being brutish you are snubbed.
And so I ask, do you think ill
of me because I have one skill?
A pair of wrestlers in a fight
will huff & puff with all their might.
The first knows many different throws
& tactics to deceive his foe,
the second only has one move
but as a ploy it always proves   *800*
victorious; with speed he scores
by dropping rivals to the floor,
& since it works why would that man
be forced to find a different plan?
You say you offer many types
of service—we are not alike—
& all your attributes combined
don't match this special skill of mine.
While hounds pursue a fox, a cat
knows how to sidestep the attack   *810*
although he only has one ruse.
The fox has many tricks to use
& thinks he'll give the dogs the slip,
but his deceits aren't up to it.

Vor he can paþes riȝte & woȝe,
an he kan hongi bi þe boȝe,
an so forlost þe hund his fore,
an turnþ aȝen eft to þan more.
Þe uox kan crope bi þe heie,
an turne ut from his forme weie,   820
an eft sone kume þarto:
þonne is þe hundes smel fordo:
he not, þur[ȝ] þe imeinde smak,
weþer he shal auorþ þe abak.
Ȝif þe uox mist of al þis dwole,
at þan ende he cropþ to hole:
ac naþeles mid alle his wrenche,
ne kan he hine so biþenche,
þeȝ he bo ȝep an suþe snel,
þat he ne lost his rede uel.   830
Þe cat ne kan wrench bute anne
noþer bi dune ne bi uenne:
bute he kan climbe suþe wel,
þarmid he wereþ his greie uel.
Al so ich segge bi mi solue,
betere is min on þan þine twelue."

"Abid! abid!" þe ule seide,
"þu gest al to mid swikelede:
alle þine wordes þu bileist
þat hit þincþ soþ al þat þu seist;   840
alle þine wordes boþ isliked,
an so bisemed an biliked,
þat alle þo þat hi auoþ,

58

He knows paths straight & crooked, how
to dangle from a branch or bough
until the hound gives up the trail
&—heading for the moor—turns tail.
The fox can creep along the hedge
& knows how best to slink & edge   *820*
down different tracks, then double back
to bring confusion, till the pack
has lost its bearings & is sent
in all directions from the scent.
His twists & turns being done, that's when
the fox heads for his earthen den,
& yet for all his crafty ways
his clever scheming never pays;
he's fast & fleet, but he'll be caught
& ripped out of his red fur coat.   *830*
The cat's one skill will never fail:
both on the hill & in the vale
he climbs up trees with such aplomb
his gray pelt stays where it belongs!
All this holds true about myself,
my single skill defeats your twelve."

"Hold on, hold on," exclaimed the Owl,
"your arguments are false & foul.
You offer such a clever spoof
it sounds as if you speak the truth,   *840*
& deal in verbal trickery
so plausible & slippery
that every individual

hi weneþ þat þu segge soþ.
Abid! abid! me shal þe ȝene.
[N]u hit shal w[u]rþe wel isene
þat þu hauest muchel iloȝe,
wone þi lesing boþ unwroȝe.
Þu seist þat þu singist mankunne,
& techest hom þat hi fundieþ hone   *850*
vp to þe songe þat eure ilest:
ac hit is alre w[u]nder mest,
þat þu darst liȝe so opeliche.
Wenest þu hi bringe so liȝtliche
to Godes riche al singin[d]e?
Nai! nai! hi shulle wel auinde
þat hi mid longe wope mote
of hore sunnen bidde bote,
ar hi mote euer kume þare.
Ich rede þi þat men bo ȝare,   *860*
an more wepe þane singe,
þat fundeþ to þan houen-kinge:
vor nis no man witute sunne.
Vorþi he mot, ar he wende honne,
mid teres an mid wope bete,
þat him bo sur þat er was swete.
Þarto ich helpe, God hit wot!
Ne singe i[c]h hom no foliot:
for al m[i] song is of longinge,
an imend sumdel mid woninge,   *870*
þat mon bi me hine biþenche
þat he gro[ni] for his unwrenche:
mid mine songe ich hine pulte,

believes your every syllable!
But wait a while. *I'll* be believed
when I describe how you deceive
& fabricate, & I'll expose
your way of speaking as a hoax.
You boast you lead the human race
with song toward some higher place   *850*
where singing happens ceaselessly,
and this is what displeases me,
this flabbergasting fib, this boast
of acting as some special host
to God's estate with just a tune.
No, no, they'll find out soon
how much they have to pray & cry
to seek redemption from their crimes
before they get to enter there,
& I advise them to prepare,   *860*
insisting they must weep, not sing,
before their journey can begin.
Before they leave their earthly home
all men, as sinners, should atone
through crying, till the tears they weep
make bitter what they thought was sweet.
God knows I sing because I'm fair
& not to catch men in a snare.
My song of longing carries tones
of lamentations in its notes,   *870*
so man will know his crimes & grieve
his misdemeanors; he'll believe
the song I'm singing, urging him

þat he groni for his gulte.
ȝif þu gest herof to disputinge,
ich wepe bet þane þu singe:
ȝif riȝt goþ forþ, & abak wrong,
betere is mi wop þane þi song.
Þeȝ sume men bo þurȝut gode,
an þurȝut clene on hore mode,   *880*
ho[m] longeþ honne noþeles.
Þat boþ her, [w]o is hom þes:
vor þeȝ hi bon hom solue iborȝe,
hi ne soþ her nowiȝt bote sorwe.
Vor oþer men hi wepeþ sore,
an for hom biddeþ Cristes ore.
Ich helpe monne on eiþer halue,
mi muþ haueþ tweire kunne salue:
þan gode ich fulste to longinge,
vor þan hi[m] longeþ, ich him singe: *890*
an þan sunfulle ich helpe alswo,
vor ich him teche þare is wo.
Ȝet ich þe ȝene in oþer wise:
vor þane þu sittest on þine rise,
þu draȝst men to fleses luste,
þat w[u]lleþ þine songes luste.
Al þu forlost þe murȝþe of houene,
for þarto neuestu none steuene:
al þat þu singst is of golnesse,
for nis on þe non holinesse,   *900*
ne wene[þ] na man for þi pipinge
þat eni preost in chir[ch]e singe.
Ȝet I þe wulle an o[þ]er segge,

to own his guilt & mourn his sins.
Disputing it won't change a thing,
I blubber better than you sing,
& right will triumph over wrong—
my weeping's better than your song.
And while some citizens are kind,
good in their hearts & pure of mind,   *880*
they pine to leave this earthly sphere,
regretting their existence here;
as people they are saved, & yet
they see a world of woe, & shed
their salty tears for other men
& pray Christ's mercy reaches them.
I help both good & bad because
my mouth brings balm to either cause.
I aid the good when longing burns
by singing to them while they yearn,   *890*
& sing to sinning men as well
to show them all where sorrows dwell.
I counter you, & will besmirch
your claims. While singing from your perch
you conjure sordid visions in
the minds of those men listening,
& lose your right to heaven's bliss
because your tune is heaven-less,
& lacking holiness you sing
of lewdness & no other thing.   *900*
No one mistakes your whistled cry
for priestly chants in church. And I
have yet another charge to lay—

ʒif þu hit const ariht bilegge:
[w]i nultu singe an o[þ]er þeode,
þar hit is muchele more neode?
Þu neauer ne singst in Irlonde,
ne þu ne cumest noʒt in Scotlonde.
Hwi nultu fare to Noreweie,
an singin men of Galeweie?
Þar beoð men þat lutel kunne
of songe þat is bineoð þe sunne.
Wi nultu þare preoste singe,
an teche of þire writelinge,
an wisi hom mid þire steuene
hu engeles singeð ine heouene?
Þu farest so doð an ydel wel
þat springeþ bi burue þa[t] is snel,
an let fordrue þe dune,
& flo[þ] on idel þar adune.
Ac ich fare boþe norþ & s[u]þ:
in eauereuch londe ich am cuuþ:
east & west, feor & neor,
I do wel faire mi meoster,
an warni men mid mine bere,
þat þi dweole-song heo ne forlere.
Ich wisse men mid min[e] songe,
þat hi ne sunegi nowiht longe:
I bidde hom þat heo iswike,
þat [heo] heom seolue ne biswike:
for betere is þat heo wepen here,
þan elles hwar [beon] deoulene fere."

910

920

930

let's see you argue this away.
Why don't you sing on foreign ground
where there's a need for such a sound?
In Ireland's realms you never call
or visit Scotland's lands at all,
nor Norway's, & don't serenade
the populace of Galloway.   910
Of any song beneath the sun
what knowledge have those people? None.
Why won't you use your songs to reach
those unenlightened priests, & teach
the clergy with your singing voice
how angels in the heavens rejoice?
You're like a useless spring that teems
close by a swiftly rushing stream
but leaves the hill-slopes dehydrated,
flowing off, entirely wasted.   920
North & south I travel &
they know of me in every land.
Both near & distant, east & west
I do again what I do best
which is to cry out in alarm
about your song's deluding charm.
I caution people, when I sing,
to guard against excessive sin;
in fact, I urge them all to stop
before they tie themselves in knots.   930
I preach that now's the time to weep,
not next time, in the devil's keep!"

Þe niȝtingale was igr[amed]
an ek heo was sum del of[s]chamed,
for þe hule hire atwiten hadde
in hwucche stude he sat an gradde,
bihinde þe bure, among þe wede,
þar men goð to here neode:
an sat sum-del, & heo biþohte,
an wiste wel on hire þohte   940
þe wraþþe binimeþ monnes red.
For hit seide þe king Alfred:
"Sel[d]e endeð wel þe loþe,
an selde plaideð wel þe wroþe."
For wraþþe meinþ þe horte blod
þat hit floweþ so wilde flod,
an al þe heorte ouergeþ,
þat heo naueþ no þing bute breþ,
an so forleost al hire liht,
þat heo ni siþ soþ ne riht.   950
Þe niȝtingale hi understod,
an ouergan lette hire mod:
he mihte bet speken a-sele
þan mid wraþþe wordes deale.

"[H]ule," heo seide "lust nu hider:
þu schalt falle, þe wei is slider.
Þu seist ich fleo bihinde bure:
hit is riht, þe bur is ure:
þar lauerd liggeþ & lauedi,
ich schal heom singe & sitte bi.   960
Wenstu þat uise men forlete,

The Nightingale was now inflamed,
& not a little bit ashamed,
because the Owl had dared to scorn
the perching site where she performed:
behind the loo, among the weeds,
where people crap & people pee.
She mulled things over for a while,
being well aware of, how, when riled,   940
a man is prone to lose his mind.
For as King Alfred once opined:
"The voice of hate is doomed to fail,
& anger pleads to no avail."
Because when rage stirs up the blood
it surges in a frenzied flood,
& overwhelms the heart until
all reason clouds, all senses fill
with darkness, & without a light
the mind is blind to truth & right.   950
Accordingly, the Nightingale
kept calm, & did not shout or wail;
she'd make a stronger argument
if she controlled her temperament.

"Now listen to me, Owl," she said,
"since it's a slippy slope you tread.
You say we skulk behind the house:
it's true, that territory's ours,
for where a lord & lady lie
we perch & sing our songs close by.   960
Do you believe the wise man should

67

for fule venne, þe riʒtte strete?
ne sunne þe later shine,
þeʒ hit bo ful ine nest[e] þine?
Sholde ich, for one hole brede,
forlete mine riʒte stede,
þat ich ne singe bi þe bedde,
þar louerd haueþ his loue ibedde?
Hit is mi riʒt, hit is mi laʒe,
þa[t] to þe he[x]st ich me draʒe.
Ac ʒet þu ʒelpst of þine songe,
þat þu canst ʒolle wroþe & stronge,
an seist þu uisest mankunne,
þat hi biwepen hore sunne.
Solde euch mon wonie & grede
riʒt suich hi weren unlede,
solde hi ʒollen al so þu dest,
hi miʒte oferen here brost.
Man schal bo stille & noʒt grede;
he mot biwepe his misdede:
ac þar is Cristes heriinge,
þar me shal grede & lude singe.
Nis noþer to lud ne to long,
at riʒte time, chirche-song.
Þu ʒolst & wones[t], & ich singe:
þi steuene is wop, & min skentinge.
Euer mote þu ʒolle & wepen
þat þu þi lif mote forleten!
an ʒollen mote þu so heʒe
þat ut berste bo þin eʒe!
Weþer is betere of twe[n]e twom,

970

980

990

68

avoid the true road due to mud?
Or that tomorrow's sun won't shine
because you nest in layers of grime?
Why would a hole cut in a seat
encourage me to seek retreat
from singing in the very place
where lord & ladyship embrace?
It is my duty & my right
to live at such a lofty height. 970
And yet you boast about your song,
claim it's so striking & so strong
it urges humans to repent
by ululating their lament.
Should people holler their distress
as if resigned to hopelessness?
Because if every person screeched
like you they'd terrify the priest.
Man should be calm & bite his tongue
& quietly confess his wrongs, 980
& only when the Lord is praised
should songs be sung & voices raised;
in church, at fitting hours, no song
can ever be too loud or long.
Your voice is filled with tears & gloom,
I sing a joyous & delightful tune.
You might well carry on & cry
relentlessly, until you die,
continuing to bawl & shout
till both your eyes come bursting out. 990
Which man is best, do you believe,

þat mon bo bliþe oþer grom?
So bo hit euer in unker siþe,
þat þu bo sori & ich bliþe.
Ʒut þu aisheist wi ich ne fare
into oþer londe & singe þare?
No! wat sholde ich among hom do,
þar neuer blisse ne com to?
Þat lond nis god, ne hit nis este,
ac wildernisse hit is & weste:
knarres & cludes houen[e]-tinge,
snou & haʒel hom is genge.
Þat lond is grislich & unuele,
þe men boþ wilde & unisele,
hi nabbeþ noþer griþ ne sibbe:
hi ne reccheþ hu hi libbe.
Hi eteþ fihs an flehs unsode,
suich wulues hit hadde tobrode:
hi drinkeþ milc & wei þarto,
hi nute elles þat hi do
hi nabbeþ noþ[er] win ne bor,
ac libbeþ al so wilde dor:
hi goþ bitiʒt mid ruʒe uelle,
riʒt suich hi comen ut of helle.
Þeʒ eni god man to hom come,
so wile dude sum from Rome,
for hom to lere gode þewes,
an for to leten hore unþewes,
he miʒte bet sitte stille,
vor al his wile he sholde spille:
he miʒte bet teche ane bore

the glad man or the man of grief?
Our lives could be described like this:
your life of glumness, mine of bliss.
You also fail to understand
why I don't sing in foreign lands.
No thanks! What joy could I provoke
in such morose & gloomy folk?
Those ugly realms are formed of tracts
of wilderness, where rocks & crags   1000
reach skyward, & whose people know
of little more than hail & snow.
Such horrible & wretched lands
breed savage, melancholy clans,
who have no harmony or peace
in their disordered tribes, & feast
on bloody fish & meat that looks
like wolf-torn flesh, & from their cups
they glug down both the whey & milk.
They lack enlightenment, that ilk   1010
who brew no beer or wine, whose lives
are feral & uncivilized,
who go about in shaggy pelts
as if they'd wandered out of hell.
The good man, heading for their home
(as one did recently, from Rome)
to teach the sinful & depraved
how decent, upright folk behave
might just as well stay put, because
he'll waste time on a fruitless cause.   1020
Far easier to teach a bear

to weʒe boþe sheld & spere,
þan me þat wilde folc ibringe
þat hi [me] wolde ihere singe.
Wat sol[d]ich þar mid mine songe?
ne sunge ich hom neuer so longe,
mi song were ispild ech del:
for hom ne mai halter ne bridel
bringe vrom hore w[o]de wise,
ne mon mid stele ne mid i[s]e.   1030
Ac war lon[d] is boþe este & god,
an þar men habbeþ milde mod,
ich noti mid hom mine þrote,
vor ich mai do þar gode note:
an bringe hom loue tiþinge,
vor ich of chirche-songe singe.
Hit was iseid in olde laʒe,
an ʒet ilast þilke soþ-saʒe,
þat man shal erien an sowe,
þar he wenþ after sum god mowe: 1040
for he is wod þat soweþ his sed
þar neuer gras ne sprinþ ne bled.”

Þe hule was wroþ, to cheste rad,
mid þisse worde hire eʒen abrad:
“Þu seist þu witest manne bures,
þar leues boþ & faire flores,
þar two iloue in one bedde
liggeþ biclop[t] & wel bihedde.
Enes þu sunge, ic wo[t] wel ware,
bi one bure, & woldest lere   1050

72

to hold a shield & hurl a spear
than kindle in that motley throng
the least desire to hear my song.
My efforts there won't change a thing;
however many hours I sing
those savages will never alter,
not if bridle nor if halter
brought their habits to an end
or steel & iron threatened them.   1030
And yet in pleasant, calmer climes
where natives think with saner minds
I exercise my vocal cords.
Such worthy work brings great reward
to those who listen to my hymns;
the church's songs are what I sing.
The ancient statutes used to say
(with wisdom that holds true today)
that man should only plant a field
on soil that brings a healthy yield;   1040
it's lunacy to plow & sow
where crops & flowers will not grow."

The angry Owl was so provoked
her eyes grew wider as she spoke.
"You claim to guard the bower where
the leaves grow & the flowers flare
& couples sleep, that sheltered place
where lovers lie down & embrace.
But once you sang—I know for sure—
outside a marriage suite, to lure   1050

þe lefdi to an uuel luue,
an sunge boþe loȝe & buue,
an lerdest hi to don shome
an vnriȝt of hire licome.
Þe louerd þat sone underȝat,
liim & grine [&] wel eiwat,
sette & le[i]de þe for to lacche.
Þu come sone to þan hacche,
þu were inume in one grine,
al hit aboȝte þine shine: 1060
þu naddest non oþer dom ne laȝe,
bute mid wilde horse were todraȝe.
Vonde ȝif þu miȝt eft misrede,
waþer þu wult, wif þe maide:
þi song mai bo so longe genge
þat þu shalt wippen on a sprenge."

Þe niȝtingale at þisse worde,
mid sworde an mid speres orde,
ȝif ho mon were, wolde fiȝte:
ac þo ho bet do ne miȝte,   1070
ho uaȝt mid hire wise tunge.
"Wel fiȝt þat wel specþ," seiþ in þe songe.
Of hire tunge ho nom red:
"Wel fiȝt þat wel specþ" seide Alured.

"Wat! seistu þis for mine shome?
þe louerd hadde herof grame.
He was so gelus of his wiue,
þat he ne miȝte for his liue

74

a lady into wicked ways.
To lead her body to disgrace
you sang tunes of a shameful sort
& filled her dreams with carnal thoughts.
His lordship soon became aware;
with lime & every type of snare
he laid his traps to make a catch,
&, landing at the window's hatch
you came to justice, being pinned
& fastened firmly by your shins.   1060
The punishment your crime would bring:
wild horses tore you limb from limb.
So do your worst with maids & wives
by bringing ruin to their lives;
your tongue will prove the very trap
that leaves you floored & in a flap."

The Nightingale, piqued at these words,
would readily have fought with swords
& spears if she had been a man,
but since she had no choice her plan   1070
involved her sharp & clever tongue.
"Who speaks well . . . fights well," goes the song;
she'd wage war with her voice instead.
"To fight well, speak well," Alfred said.

"Your talk won't cover me in shame—
his lordship was the one to blame
for being jealous of his wife.
His envy could have cost his life

75

iso þat man wiþ hire speke,
þat his horte nolde breke.
He hire bileck in one bure,
þat hire was boþe stronge & sure:
ich hadde of hire milse an ore,
an sori was for hire sore,
an skente hi mid mine songe
al þat ich miȝte, raþe an longe.
Vorþan þe kniȝt was wiþ me wroþ,
vor riȝte niþe ich was him loþ:
he dude me his oȝene shome,
ac al him turnde it to grome.
Þat underyat þe king Henri:
Jesus his soule do merci!
He let forbonne þene kniȝt,
þat hadde idon so muchel unriȝt
ine so gode kinges londe;
vor riȝte niþe & for fule onde
let þane lutle fuȝel nime
an him fordeme lif an lime.
Hit was w[u]rþsipe al mine kunne;
forþon þe kniȝt forles his wunne,
an ȝaf for me an hundred punde:
an mine briddes seten isunde,
an hadde soþþe blisse & hiȝte,
an were bliþe, & wel miȝte.
Vorþon ich was so wel awreke,
euer eft ich dar[r] þe bet speke:
vor hit bitidde ene swo,
ich am þe bliþur euer mo.

1080

1090

1100

because his heart began to fail
when she conversed with other males.
He locked her in an inner chamber;
strong & steadfast bounds contained her;
sorry for her anguish there
I felt her pain & pitied her
& kept her cheerful all day long
by filling every hour with song,
a tactic that enraged the knight
who loathed my bones with all his might.
He tried to make his problem mine
but was found guilty of the crime:
on hearing of that man's misdeed
King Henry, rest in peace, decreed
the sentence must be banishment,
a right & proper punishment
for acts so base & underhand
committed in a good king's land,
whereby a tiny Nightingale
had been dismembered top to tail.
To bring back honor to my race
he wiped the smile from that man's face
& made him pay one hundred pounds
to me. My chicks, now safe & sound,
enjoy their new prosperity
by right, & their security.
And I, avenged of the offense,
speak with a strengthened confidence.
Because of that one incident
my cheerfulness is permanent

Nu ich mai singe war ich wulle,
ne dar me neuer eft mon agrulle.
Ac þu, eremi[n]g! þu wrecche gost!
þu ne canst finde, ne þu nost,
an holʒ stok þar þu þe miʒt hude,
þat me ne twengeþ þine hude.
Vor children, gromes, heme & hine,
hi þencheþ alle of þire pine:
ʒif hi muʒe iso þe sitte,
stones hi doþ in hore slitte,
an þe totorue[þ] & toheneþ,
an þine fule bon tosheneþ.
ʒif þu art iworpe oþer ishote,
þanne þu miʒt erest to note.
Vor me þe hoþ in one rodde,
an þu, mid þine fule codde,
an mid þine ateliche s[w]ore,
biwerest manne corn urom dore.
Nis noþer noʒt, þi lif ne þi blod:
ac þu art sh[e]ueles suþe god.
Þar nowe sedes boþe isowe,
pinnuc, golfinc, rok, ne crowe
ne dar þar neuer cumen ihende,
ʒif þi buc hongeþ at þan ende.
Þar tron shulle aʒere blowe,
an ʒunge sedes springe & growe,
ne dar no fuʒel þarto uonge,
ʒif þu art þarouer ihonge.
Þi lif is eure luþer & qued,
þu nar[t] noʒt bute ded.

& as I please I raise my voice
& no one dares dispute my choice. 1110
But you, you wretch, you ghoulish ghost,
you can't identify a post
or hollow stump to crouch inside
avoiding those who'd nip your hide.
For youngsters, serfs, & those who farm,
& peasant folk, all mean you harm,
& if they spy you on your perch
they hope to injure you, or worse,
& fill their pockets up with stones
then aim to break your horrid bones. 1120
It's only when you're struck or shot
that people find your body's got
some kind of use: your loathsome neck
& trunk, hung on a stick, deflect
all kinds of hungry birds & beasts
who eye man's corn crops as their feast.
There's no worth in your flesh & blood
though as a scarecrow you're quite good
wherever seeds are newly sown,
for sparrow, goldfinch, rook & crow 1130
will never venture near the clod
where your corpse dangles from a rod.
Each springtime, when the blossom's out
& young seeds germinate then sprout,
no famished bird would ever dare
go near them if you're swinging there.
You're vile & foul when drawing breath
& only valuable in death.

Nu þu miȝt wite sikerliche
þat þine leches boþ grisliche
þe wile þu art on lifdaȝe:
vor wane þu hongest islaȝe,
ȝut hi boþ of þe ofdradde,
þe fuȝeles þat þe er bigradde.
Mid riȝte men boþ wiþ þe wroþe,
for þu singist euer of hore loþe:
al þat þu singst, raþe oþer late,
hit is euer of manne unwate:
wane þu hauest aniȝt igrad,
men boþ of þe wel sore ofdrad.
Þu singst þar sum man shal be ded:
euer þu bodest sumne qued.
Þu singst aȝen eiȝte lure,
oþer of summe frondes rure:
oþer þu bodes[t] huses brune,
oþer ferde of manne, oþer þoues rune;
oþer þu bodest cualm of oreue,
oþer þat londfolc wurþ idorue,
oþer þat wif lost hire make;
oþer þu bodest cheste an sake.
Euer þu singist of manne hareme,
þurȝ þe hi boþ sori & areme.
þu ne singst neuer one siþe,
þat hit nis for sum unsiþe.
Heruore hit is þat me þe shuneþ,
an þe totorueþ & tobuneþ
mid staue, & stoone, & turf, & clute,
þat þu ne miȝt nowar atrute.

So now it's irrefutable
that you are far from beautiful 1140
when you're alive, because those birds,
who shrieked when your grim form disturbed
their eyes, are still spooked by your looks
when you're deceased & on a hook.
You're viewed with scorn, & rightly so,
for always singing songs of woe,
reminding folk of things they hate
from early morning until late.
Your terrifying call gives fright
to those who hear it in the night. 1150
Your cry's a sign of certain doom:
it says a man will perish soon
or lose his property, or spells
the ruin of a friend, foretells
a house-fire, or of being mobbed
by violent thugs, or being robbed,
or hints at plague among the herd,
or human sickness, or brings word
that widowhood awaits the wife,
or points to conflict & to strife. 1160
You sing of human strain & stress—
all those who hear you feel depressed—
& never sing at all unless
you're trumpeting some great distress.
And therefore, you are vilified;
you're thrashed & pelted, folks let fly
with sticks & stones & sods & peat
until there's nowhere to retreat.

Dahet euer suich budel in tune
þat euer bodeþ unwreste rune,   1170
an euer bringeþ vuele tiþinge,
an þat euer specþ of vuele þinge!
God Almiȝti w[u]rþe him wroþ,
an al þat werieþ linnene cloþ!"

Þe hule ne abo[d] noȝt swiþ[e] longe,
ah ȝef ondsware starke & stronge:
"Wat," quaþ ho, "hartu ihoded?
oþer þu kursest al unihoded?
For prestes wike ich wat þu dest.
Ich not ȝef þu were ȝaure prest: 1180
ich not ȝef þu canst masse singe:
inoh þu canst of mansinge.
Ah hit is for þine alde niþe,
þat þu me akursedest oþer siþe:
ah þarto is lihtlich ondsware;
'Drah to þe!' cwaþ þe cartare.
Wi attwitestu me mine insihte,
an min iwit & mine miȝte?
For ich am witi ful iwis,
an wo[t] al þat to kumen is: 1190
ich wot of hunger, of hergonge:
ich wot ȝef men schule libbe longe:
ich wat ȝef wif lus[t] hire make:
ich wat þar schal beo niþ & wrake;
ich wot hwo schal beon [an]honge,
oþer elles fulne deþ afonge.
Ȝef men habbeþ bataile inume,

You're like a cursed town-crier who's
forever spouting sorry news,   1170
a herald with an evil cry
whose proclamations terrify.
May you be subject to the wrath
of all those wearing linen cloth."

The Owl did not delay for long,
her answer came back loud & strong.
"Have you become ordained? You preach
without the backing of the priest,
& act as though you are a priest,
which you are not, not in the least!   1180
I never heard you sing the Mass
& yet you curse at will, & pass
snide comments, blackening my name
through malice, time & time again.
To which there is a swift reply:
'Move over,' is the carter's cry.
Why does my power, wit & vision
draw from you such crude derision?
I am wise & no mistake,
& know which paths the future takes.   1190
I forecast famine, war, the age
a person will achieve, & gauge
when wives will lose their husbands, &
when vengeful strife will haunt the land.
I know who'll dangle from a noose,
who'll meet a grisly end, who'll lose
their life in combat—hear the call

ich wat hwaþer schal beon ouerkume:
ich wat ȝif cwalm scal comen on orfe,
an ȝif dor schul ligge [a]storue;   1200
ich wot ȝef treon schule blowe:
ich wat ȝef cornes schule growe:
ich wot ȝef huses schule berne:
ich wot ȝef men schule eorne oþer erne:
ich wot ȝef sea schal schipes drenche:
ich wot ȝef snuw[e] schal uuele clenche.
An ȝet ich con muchel more:
ich con inoh in bokes lore,
an eke ich can of þe Goddspelle
more þan ich nule þe telle: 1210
for ich at chirche come ilome,
an muche leorni of wisdome:
ich wat al of þe tacninge,
an of oþer feole þinge.
Ȝef eni mon schal rem abide,
al ich hit wot ear hit itide.
Ofte, for mine muchele iwitte,
wel sori-mod & w[ro]þ ich sitte:
wan ich iseo þat sum wrechede
is manne neh, innoh ich grede: 1220
ich bidde þat men beon iwar[r]e,
an habbe gode reades ȝar[r]e.
For Alfred seide a wis word,
euch mon hit schulde legge on hord:
'Ȝef þu isihst [er] he beo icume,
his str[e]ncþe is him wel neh binume.'
An grete duntes beoþ þe lasse,

84

of warfare, fight their battle, fall.
Which cows will suffer from disease,
which beasts will soon be on their knees,
if trees will bloom, if corn will grow—
all of these things I know. I know
which houses will be burnt to soot,
who'll go by carriage, who on foot,
which ships will sink in heavy seas,
which smiths will rivet faulty seams.
I know all this & more besides;
through reading books I'm very wise,
& from the gospels have worked out
more than I care to talk about.   1210
I often go to church & find
the lessons there improve my mind,
therefore, the power to divine
is one of many skills of mine;
I know before the hue & cry
who's being hunted down, & why.
And yet my talent leaves me cross
& sad while sitting here, because
I see misfortune is about
to find its prey, & I cry out;   1220
I warn folk to be vigilant
& plan for future incidents.
A clever lesson Alfred taught
that should remain within our thoughts:
'A threat seen in its infancy
will lose much of its potency.'
So heavy jolts have far less force

ȝef me ikepþ mid iwarnesse,
an [flo] schal toward misȝenge,
ȝef þu isihst hu fleo of strenge;   1230
for þu miȝt blenche wel & fleo,
ȝif þu isihst heo to þe teo.
Þat eni man beo falle in [e]dwite,
wi schal he me his sor atwite?
Þah ich iseo his harm biuore,
ne comeþ hit noȝt of me þaru[o]re.
Þah þu iseo þat sum blind mon,
þat nanne rihtne wei ne con,
to þare diche his dweole fulie[þ],
an falleþ, and þarone sulie[þ]   1240
wenest þu, þah ich al iseo,
þat hit for me þe raþere beo?
Al swo hit fareþ bi mine witte:
hwanne ich on mine bowe sitte,
ich wot & iseo swiþe brihte
an summe men kume[&] harm þarrihte.
Schal he, þat þerof noþing not,
hit wite me for ich hit wot?
Schal he his mishap wite me,
for ich am wisure þane he?   1250
Hwanne ich iseo þat sum wrechede
is manne neh, inoh ich grede,
an bidde inoh þat hi heom schilde,
for toward heom is [harm unmilde].
Ah þah ich grede lude an stille,
al hit itid þur[h] Godes wille.
Hwi wulleþ men of me hi mene,

if spotted early in their course;
& you can dodge an arrow's blow
by watching as it leaves the bow,   *1230*
then keeping its approach in sight,
then ducking from its fatal flight.
And when a man encounters shame
or harm, why must I take the blame?
I know what trouble to expect
but I am not its architect.
So, if a blind man lost his way,
& you observed that fellow stray
from his intended path, & pitch
into a stinking, muddy ditch,   *1240*
don't claim the sorry consequence
was brought on by my prescience.
My mind detects things in advance,
so when I'm sitting on my branch
I know with perfect clarity
when mishap or calamity
will strike a man, but don't blame me
for seeing things that he can't see.
Should I be made to bear the blame
because I have the better brain?   *1250*
When I see misery or harm
approach I cry out in alarm,
& beg that people be on guard
before disaster hits them hard.
But if my call is soft or shrill
whatever happens is God's will.
So why do people grumble when

þah ich mid soþe heo awene?
Þah ich hi warni al þat ȝer,
nis heom þerfore harem no þe ner: 1260
ah ich heom singe for ich wolde
þat hi wel understonde schulde
þat sum unselþe heom is ihende,
hwan ich min huing to heom sende.
Naueþ no man none sikerhede
þat he ne mai wene & adrede
þat sum unhwate ne[h] him beo,
þah he ne conne hit iseo.
Forþi seide Alfred swiþe wel,
and his worde was Goddspel,   1270
þat 'euereuch man, þe bet him beo,
eauer þe bet he hine beseo':
'ne truste no mon to his weole
to swiþe, þah he habbe ueole.'
'Nis [nout] so hot þat hit nacoleþ,
ne noȝt so hwit þat hit ne soleþ,
ne noȝt so leof þat hit ne aloþeþ,
ne noȝt so glad þat hit ne awroþeþ:
ac eauereeu[c]h þing þat eche nis,
agon schal, & al þis worldes blis.'   1280
Nu þu miȝt wite readliche,
þat eauere þu spekest gideliche:
for al þat þu me seist for schame,
euer þe seolue hit turneþ to grome.
Go so hit go, at eche fenge
þu fallest mid þine ahene swenge;
al þat þu seist for me to schende,

the truth I utter troubles them?
I can't bring misadventure near
by warning of it for a year,
I sing so folk will understand
catastrophe is close at hand.
Yes, when I hoot some dark event
is heralded as imminent.
For nobody remains secure
forever; we can be assured
that danger, even when concealed,
is no less threatening or real.
King Alfred coined this fitting truth
(& his word was the gospel truth):
'The better-off the man,' he said,
'the more that man must plan ahead.'
Despite what riches might be his
a man can't trust to wealth. There is
no heat that can't go off the boil,
no purest white that can't be soiled,
no love that can't resort to hate,
no joy that can't infuriate.
Like earthly bliss all things must pass.
Eternity alone will last.
Presumably you'll now accept
your arguments lack intellect,
since all the slurs & slights you spread
return & sully you instead.
What's more, you suffer at the hand
of every punch you try to land.
Whatever your malign intent

1260

1270

1280

89

hit is mi wurschipe at þan ende.
Bute þu wille bet aginne,
ne shaltu bute schame iwinne." 1290

Þe niȝtingale sat & siȝte,
& hohful was, & ful wel miȝte,
for þe hule swo ispeke hadde,
an hire speche swo iladde.
Heo was ho[h]ful, & erede
hwat heo þarafter hire sede:
ah neoþeles heo hire understod.
"Wat!" heo seide, "hule, artu wod?
þu ȝeolpest of seolliche wisdome,
þu nustest wanene he þe come, 1300
bute hit of wicchecrefte were.
Þarof þu, wrecche, mos[t] þe skere
ȝif þu wult among manne b[eo]:
oþer þu most of londe fleo.
For alle þeo þat [þ]erof cuþe,
heo uere ifurn of prestes muþe
amanset: swuch þu art ȝette,
þu wiecche-crafte neauer ne lete.
Ich þe seide nu lutel ere,
an þu askedest ȝef ich were 1310
a-bisemere to preost ihoded.
Ah þe mansing is so ibroded,
þah no preost a-londe nere,
a wrecche neoþeles þu were:
for eauereuch chil[d] þe cleopeþ fule,
an euereuch man a wrecche hule.

90

each jibe becomes a compliment,
so start afresh, rethink your claim
or shame's the only prize you'll gain."   1290

The Nightingale was flummoxed now.
She sat & sighed, disarmed by how
the Owl had verbalized her case
& put her in an awkward place
with words that left her lost & vexed
& worried what to argue next.
But she was smart, & in exchange
replied: "What? Owl, are you deranged?
You state that you can prophesize,
but how did you become so wise?   1300
Perhaps your teacher was a witch,
a charge you'll have to answer, wretch,
to stay among the human race,
or else you'll have to flee this place.
For those who deal in mystic arts
are scorned by priests & must depart
the Faith; & since you still insist
on witchery, your ban persists.
I made this clear not long ago,
then brazenly you asked to know   1310
if I'd become a priest or not,
but people curse you such a lot
that even living in a land
devoid of priests you'd still be damned,
for children speak of you as 'foul,'
& adults as 'the worthless Owl.'

Ich habbe iherd, & soþ hit is,
þe mon mot beo wel storre-wis,
[þat] wite inno[h] of wucche þinge kume,
so þu seist þ[e] is iwune.

1320

Hwat canstu, wrecche þing, of storre,
bute þat þu biha[u]est hi feorre?
Alswo deþ mani dor & man,
þeo of [swucche] nawiht ne con.
On ape mai a boc bih[o]lde,
an leues wenden & eft folde:
ac he ne con þe bet þaruore
of clerkes lore top ne more.
Þah þu iseo þe steorre alsw[o],
nartu þe wisure neauer þe mo.

1330

Ah ʒet þu, fule þing, me chist,
an wel grimliche me atwist
þat ich singe bi manne huse,
an teache wif breke spuse.
Þu liest iwis, þu fule þing!
þ[urh] me nas neauer ischend spusing.
Ah soþ hit is ich singe & grede
þar lauedies beoþ & faire maide;
& soþ hit is of luue ich singe:
for god wif mai i[n] spusing

1340

bet luuien hire oʒene were,
þane awe[r] hire copenere;
an maide mai luue cheose
þat hire wurþschipe ne forleose,
an luuie mid rihte luue
þane þe schal beon hire buue.

I've heard that prophesy relies
on readings of the starry skies
to make predictions that come true,
as you have often claimed to do.   1320
But you know nothing of the stars,
you only watch them from afar
like any man or animal
who boasts no special oracle.
An ape can take a long hard look
at every page inside a book
then close it, & know nothing more
of any theory or law.
And you are no anomaly,
a stranger to astrology.   1330
Yet you persist with your assault,
you rogue, & say that I'm at fault
for singing close to fellows' houses,
meaning to corrupt their spouses.
But you speak dishonestly;
no marriage failed because of me,
though I admit I call & sing
to girls & women, & the thing
I sing about is love, it's true.
I want good women to pursue   1340
the love between a married pair
& not resort to an affair;
I urge young maidens not to chase
the kind of love that brings disgrace
but satisfy their hearts as wives
who love their husbands all their lives.

Swiche luue ich itache & lere,
þerof beoþ al mine ibere.
Þah sum wif beo of nesche mode,
for wumm[e]n beoþ of softe blode,   1350
þat heo, þurh sume sottes lore
þe ӡeorne bit & sikeþ sore,
mis[r]empe & misdo sumne stunde,
schal ich þaruore beon ibunde?
Ӡif wimmen luuieþ unrede,
[w]itestu me hore misdede?
Ӡef wimmon þencheþ luuie derne,
[ne] mai ich mine songes werne.
Wummon mai pleie under cloþe,
weþer heo wile, wel þe wroþe: 1360
& heo mai do bi mine songe,
hwaþer heo wule, wel þe wronge.
For nis a-worlde þing so god,
þat ne mai do sum ungod,
ӡif me hit wule turne amis.
For gold & seoluer, god hit is:
an noþeles þarmid þu miӡt
spusbruche buggen & unriӡt.
Wepne beoþ gode griþ to halde:
ah neoþeles þarmide beoþ men acwalde   1370
aӡeines riht [an] fale londe,
þar þeoues hi bereð an honde.
Alswa hit is bi mine songe,
þah heo beo god, me hine mai misfonge,
an drahe hine to sothede,
an to oþre uuele dede.

This is the message I promote,
the essence of my every note.
A woman might not have enough
resolve (being made of finer stuff) 1350
to snub a suitor's compliments
or breathless sighs; if she relents
& misbehaves with him, don't claim
the fault is mine, that I'm to blame.
If love proves women pliable
in no way am I liable;
if women plan to go astray
I'll go on singing anyway;
a woman can have fun in bed
for reasons either good or bad, 1360
& she'll interpret what I sing
as either virtue or as sin.
For there is nothing on this earth,
however notable its worth,
that can't be sullied or misused,
as gold & silver are abused
when precious metals are exchanged
for vice or mischief. This explains
why weapons—good for keeping peace—
when owned illicitly by thieves 1370
are murderous weapons in their hands,
as is the case in foreign lands.
And it's no different with my voice:
sweet as it is, it can, by choice,
be twisted from the virtuous
& used for wicked purposes.

Ah [schaltu] wrecch, luue tele?
Bo wuch ho bo, vich luue is fele
bitweone wepmon & wimmane:
ah ȝef heo is atbroide, þenne   1380
he is unfele & forbrode.
Wroþ wurþe heom þe holi rode
þe rihte ikunde swo forbreideþ!
W[u]nder hit is þat heo nawedeþ.
An swo heo doþ, for heo beoþ wode
þe bute nest goþ to brode.
Wummon is of nesche flesche,
an flesches [lust] is strong to cwesse:
nis wunder nan þah he abide.
For flesches lustes hi makeþ slide,   1390
ne beoþ heo nowt alle forlore,
þat stumpeþ at þe flesches more:
for moni wummon haueþ misdo
þat aris[t] op of þe slo.
Ne beoþ nowt ones alle sunne,
forþan hi beoþ tweire kunne:
su[m] arist of þe flesches luste,
an sum of þe gostes custe.
Þar flesch draheþ men to drunnesse,
an to [wrouehede] & to golnesse,   1400
þe gost misdeþ þurch niþe an onde,
& seoþþe mid murhþe of [monne shonde,]
an ȝeoneþ after more & more,
an lutel rehþ of milce & ore;
an stiȝþ on he[h] þur[h] modinesse,
an ouerhoheð þanne lasse.

96

But don't blame love—that's horrible.
For love is proud & honorable
between a man & woman, though
not stolen love; that love is low,   1380
the sordid, grubby type. Well may
the Holy Cross bring down its rage
on those who act unnaturally—
they must be mad. And actually
a woman is insane indeed
who goes outside the nest to breed.
A female's flesh is very frail,
no wonder she's condemned to fail
if crude desire maintains its grip,
forever causing her to slip,   1390
though they are not completely lost
who stumble on the rocks of lust;
those overtaken by desire
have often risen from the mire.
And when it comes to sin & shame
there are two different types to name:
the first is the licentious kind,
the second is a cast of mind.
The flesh leads men to drunken days
& lechery & idle ways;   1400
a troubled spirit leads to spite
& envy, & invokes delight
at men's misfortunes, fosters greed
& scoffs at kind & caring deeds,
belittles & derides the meek
& swells with pompous pride. So speak

Sei [me sooþ], ʒef þu hit wost,
hweþer deþ wurse, flesch þe gost?
Þu miʒt segge, ʒef þu wult,
þat lasse is þe flesches gult: 1410
moni man is of his flesche clene,
þat is mid mode deouel-imene.
Ne schal non mon wimman bigrede,
an flesches lustes hire upbreide:
swuch he may te[l]en of golnesse,
þat sunegeþ wurse i[n] modinesse.
[ʒ]et ʒif ich schulde a-luue bringe
wif oþer maide, hwanne ich singe,
ich wolde wiþ þe maide holde,
ʒif þu hit const ariht atholde: 1420
Lust nu, ich segge þe hwaruore,
vp to þe toppe from þe morc.
ʒef maide luueþ dernliche,
heo stumpeþ & falþ icundeliche:
for þah heo sum hwile pleie,
heo nis nout feor ut of þe weie;
heo mai hire guld atwende
a rihte weie þur[h] chirche-bende,
an mai eft habbe to make
hire leofmon wiþute sake,   1430
an go to him bi daies lihte,
þat er stal to bi þeostre nihte.
An ʒunling not hwat swuch þing is:
his ʒunge blod hit draʒeþ amis,
an sum sot mon hit tihþ þarto
mid alle þan þat he mai do.

the truth: by rank, is flesh the first
of evils, or is spirit worse?
Admit, then, if you think it's true
that flesh is least bad, of the two,   1410
since many men, their souls enmeshed
with Satan's cause, are pure of flesh.
No person should go slandering
a woman's lowly hankerings,
& he who argues from that side
commits the greater sin of pride.
Both wives & maidens, through my voice,
give in to passion, but my choice
would be the virgin every time—
your thoughts will no doubt echo mine   1420
once you have heard my argument
from its beginning to its end.
A virgin, by her nature, may
succumb to lust & lose her way
but still be lifted up & saved
no matter how she misbehaves,
because by taking marriage vows
she'll rid herself of guilt; her spouse
was once her lover, but the pair
are now excused of their affair.   1430
The man she trysted with at night
is hers now every day, by right.
A young girl doesn't understand
and so obeys her heart's commands;
the reckless fellow leads her on
with every tactic known to man:

He comeþ & fareþ & beod & bi[t]
an heo bistant & ouersi[t],
an bisehþ ilome & longe.
Hwat mai þat chil[d] þah hit misfonge? 1440
Hit nuste neauer hwat hit was,
forþi hit þohte fondi [þ]as,
an wite iwis hwuch beo þe gome
þat of so wilde makeþ tome.
Ne mai ich for reo[w]e lete,
wanne ich iseo þe tohte ilete
þe luue bring[e] on þe ȝunglinge,
þat ich of murȝþe him ne singe.
Ich [t]eache heom bi mine songe
þat swucch luue ne lest noȝt longe: 1450
for mi song lutle hwile ilest,
an luue ne deþ noȝt butc rest
on swuch childre, & sone ageþ,
an falþ adun þe hote breþ.
Ich singe mid heom one þroȝe,
biginne on heh & endi laȝe,
an lete [mine] songes falle
an lutle wile adun mid alle.
Þat maide wot, hwanne ich swike,
þat luue is mine songes ili[k]e, 1460
for hit nis bute a lutel breþ,
þat sone kumeþ, & sone geþ.
Þat child bi me hit understond,
an his unred to red[e] wend,
an iseȝþ wel, bi mine songe,
þat dusi luue ne last noȝt longe.

he comes & goes, commands & begs,
harangues her then plays hard to get,
implores her, pleads with her so long,
can she be blamed if things go wrong?   1440
She didn't know the dangers, so
she thought she'd give the thing a go,
experimenting with the game
that makes the wild & frisky tame.
Through pity, then, I can't resist,
delivering a song of bliss
when witnessing the painful trace
that love leaves in young girl's face.
I try to teach them, through my song,
love of that kind will not last long,   1450
because, just as my song relents,
love rarely stays when it descends
on children's hearts, but meets its death
the way that warmth fades on our breath.
I sing my song to them, its flow
beginning high & ending low,
until the melody subsides
and shortly afterward it dies;
on hearing that my song has passed
girls understand that love won't last,   1460
because my song's a gasp of air
that briefly lives then disappears.
Through me, young women turn
away from ignorance & learn
that dizzy passion, like my tune,
will fade away, and all too soon.

Ah wel ich wule þat þu hit wite,
loþ me beoþ wiues utschute:
ah [w]if mai [of] me nime ȝeme,
ich ne singe nawt hwan ich teme.   1470
An wif ah lete so[t]tes lore,
þah spusing-bendes þuncheþ sore.
Wundere me þungþ wel starc & stor,
hu eni mon so eauar for,
þat [h]e his heorte miȝte driue
[to] do hit to oþers mannes wiue:
for oþer hit is of twam þinge,
ne mai þat þridde no man bringe;
o[þ]ar þe lauerd is wel aht,
oþer aswunde, & nis naht.   1480
Ȝef he is wurþful & aht man,
nele no man, þat wisdo[m] can,
hure of is wiue do him schame:
for he mai him adrede grame,
an þat he forleose þat þer hongeþ,
þat him eft þarto noȝt ne longeþ.
An þah he þat noȝt ne adrede,
hit is unriȝt & gret sothede
[to] misdon one gode manne,
an his ibedde from him spanne.   1490
Ȝef hire lauerd is forwurde
an unorne at bedde & at borde,
hu miȝte þar beo eni luue
wanne [a] cheorles buc hire ley buue?
Hu mai þar eni luue beo,
war swuch man gropeþ hire þeo?

102

Believe me, though, I'm horrified
when married women cheat & lie.
A wife should note: I sing no song
while I am pregnant with my young.   1470
A marriage might be firmly forged
but flirty fools should be ignored;
I am both sickened & amazed
that men, at times, are so depraved
they have the nerve to go to bed
with someone else's wife instead.
Two explanations I have heard
& will relate, but not a third:
the husband here is either brave
or he's a weak & worthless knave.   1480
If he's a bold & manly sort
nobody with a brain would court
his wife until she parts her legs;
that fool would end up hurt or dead
or lose what dangles from his groin
& never feel desire again!
And even if he's not afraid
it's still a dirty, low-down trade,
offending decent gentlemen
by sleeping with their wives. And then   1490
we have the other sort, inept
with food & worse in bed; expect
no love when men so grossly fat
roll on their wives & squash them flat,
when oafs like that reach for their wives
to grope & fumble at their thighs.

Herbi þu miȝt wel understonde
þat on [is a reu], þat oþer schonde,
to stele to oþres mannes bedde.
For ȝif aht man is hire bedde,   1500
þu miȝt wene þat þe mistide,
wanne þu list bi hire side.
An ȝef þe lauerd is a w[re]cche,
hwuch este miȝtistu þar uecche?
Ȝif þu biþenchest hwo hire ofligge,
þu miȝt mid wlate þe este bugge.
Ich not hu mai eni freo-man
for hire sechen after þan.
Ȝef he biþencþ bi hwan he lai,
al mai þe luue gan awai."   1510

Þe hule was glad of swuche tale:
heo þoȝte þat te nihtegale,
þah heo wel speke atte frume,
hadde at þen ende misnume:
an seide: "Nu ich habbe ifunde
þat maidenes beoþ of þine imunde:
mid heom þu holdest, & heom biwerest,
an ouerswiþe þu hi herest.
Þe lauedies beoþ to me iwend,
to me heo hire mo[n]e send.   1520
For hit itit ofte & ilome,
þat wif & were beoþ unisome:
& þerfore þe were gulte,
þat leof is over wummon to pulte,
an speneþ on þare al þat he haueþ,

104

So, of those two adulteries
the first results in injury,
the second in embarrassment;
through acts of brutal harassment   *1500*
the husband who is tough will harm
the man who takes his woman's arm,
but if her man's a wretch it must
reduce the lover to disgust,
imagining the worthless dregs
who've writhed between the woman's legs.
No man with any self-respect
could sleep with her, should he reflect
what types she's entertained before;
no love would last there anymore."   *1510*

The Owl was glad to hear this tale,
because although the Nightingale
had started speaking well enough
her argument had tapered off.
She said, "From what you have described
it's clear your sympathies reside
with girls; they're faultless in your eyes,
therefore, you praise them to the skies.
But married women, filled with grief,
all turn to me to seek relief.   *1520*
It happens time & time again
that married life comes under strain,
because of which the husband strays
& finds some other love to chase,
immorally pursuing her

an siueþ þare þat no riht naueþ,
an haueþ attom his riȝte spuse,
wowes weste, & lere huse,
wel þunne isch[r]ud & iued wroþe,
an let heo bute mete & cloþe. 1530
Wan he comeþ ham eft to his wiue,
ne dar heo noȝt a word ischire:
he chid & gred swuch he beo wod,
an ne bringþ [hom] non oþer god.
Al þat heo deþ him is unwille,
al þat heo spekeþ hit is him ille:
an oft hwan heo noȝt ne misdeþ,
heo haueþ þe fust in hire teþ.
Þ[er] is nan mon þat ne mai ibringe
his wif amis mid swucche þinge: 1540
me hire mai so ofte misbeode,
þat heo do wule hire ahene neode.
La, Godd hit wot! heo nah iweld,
þa[h] heo hine makie kukeweld.
For hit itit lome & ofte,
þat his wif is wel nesche & softe,
of faire bleo & wel idiht:
[For]þi hit is þe more unriht
þat he his luue spene on þare,
þat nis wurþ one of hire heare. 1550
An swucche men beoþ wel manifolde,
þat wif ne kunne noȝt ariȝt holde.
Ne mot non mon wiþ hire speke:
he ueneð heo wule anon tobreke
hire spusing, ȝef heo lokeþ

& tipping out his purse on her,
abandoning his lawful spouse
who occupies their lonely house
in threadbare clothes, among bare walls,
with very little food at all.   1530
And out of terror she has learned
to bite her lip once he's returned,
though like a lunatic he shouts
& bawls & throws his weight about.
All that she does displeases him,
all that she utters teases him,
& when she tries to keep the peace
he's apt to punch her in the teeth.
The man who misbehaves that way
can't fail to send his wife astray.   1540
Because of his abuse at home
she'll seek out pleasures of her own;
she'll cuckold him, of course she will,
but don't say she's responsible.
And yes, it's usually the case
she's well brought-up & fair of face,
so when the husband spends his purse
outside the home the crime seems worse—
the mistress of his love affair
is barely worth one strand of hair   1550
belonging to his spouse. In life
such husbands fail to trust their wives:
no other men must talk to them,
& if they look at other men
or speak with other men politely

oþer wiþ manne faire spekeþ.
He hire bilu[k]þ mid keie & loke:
þar-þurh is spusing ofte tobroke.
For ȝef heo is þarto ibroht,
he deþ þat heo nadde ear iþoht.
Dahet þat to swuþe hit bispeke,
þah swucche wiues [heom] awreke!
Herof þe lauedies to me meneþ,
an wel sore me ahweneþ:
wel neh min heorte wule tochine,
hwon ich biholde hire pine.
Mid heom ich wepe swi[þ]e sore,
an for heom bidde Cristis ore,
þat þe lauedi sone aredde
an hire sende betere ibedde.
An oþer þing ich mai þe telle,
þat þu ne schal[t], for þine felle,
ondswere none þarto finde:
al þi sputing schal aswinde.
Moni chapmon & moni cniht
luueþ & [hald] his wif ariht,
an swa deþ moni bondeman:
þat gode wif deþ after þan,
an serueþ him to bedde & to borde
mid faire dede & faire worde,
an ȝeorne fondeþ hu heo muhe
do þing þat him beo iduȝe.
Þe lauerd into þare [þ]eode
fareþ ut on þare beire nede,
an is þat gode wif unbliþe

1560

1570

1580

husbands think deceit is likely.
Stifled, then, by lock & key,
the wives turn to adultery,
because they're driven to explore
what was anathema before.   1560
A curse on those who whine & whinge
when wives deliver their revenge.
This is the thing that wives complain
to me about; I feel their pain
& sense such overwhelming hurt
I sometimes think my heart will burst.
My eyes are sore with bitter tears;
I pray that Christ our Lord will hear
their prayers so wives might share their beds
with decent, honest men instead.   1570
And now I'll tell you one thing more
that you will have no answer for,
I'll put your logic in a spin
& no reply will save your skin.
So, many merchants, many knights,
will love their wives & treat them right,
& many peasants will do too;
accordingly each wife stays true,
& does her best to serve her lord
both in the bedroom & at board   1580
& eagerly she'll aim to please
with caring words & thoughtful deeds.
The husband travels far & wide
in his endeavors to provide
for them, & when he ups & leaves

for hire lauerdes hou[h]siþe,
an sit & sihð wel sore oflonged,
an hire sore an horte ongred:
al for hire louerdes sake
haueþ daies kare & niȝtes wake: 1590
an swuþe longe hire is þe hwile,
an [ech] steape hire þunþ a mile.
Hwanne oþre slepeþ hire abute,
ich one lust þar wiþute,
an wot of hire sore mode,
an singe aniȝt for hire gode:
an mine gode song, for hire þinge,
ich turne su[m]del to murni[n]ge.
Of hure seorhe ich bere sume,
forþan ich am hire wel welcume: 1600
ich hire helpe hwat [I] mai,
for [ho geþ] þane rehte wai.
Ah þu me hauest sore igramed,
þat min heorte is wel neh alamed,
þat ich mai unneaþe speke:
ah ȝet ich wule forþure reke.
Þu seist þat ich am manne [lo&],
an euereuch man is wið me wroð,
an me mid stone & lugge þreteþ,
an me tobu[r]steþ & tobeteþ, 1610
an hwanne heo hab[b]eþ me ofslahe,
heo hongeþ me on heore hahe,
þar ich aschewele pie an crowe
fro[m] þan þe þar is isowe.
Þah hit beo soþ, ich do heom god,

110

the steadfast wife at home will grieve;
she'll sit & sigh when he departs
because a longing fills her heart
&, anxious for her husband's sake,
she'll fret by day then lie awake;   1590
each moment lasts a long, long while,
& every step feels like a mile.
Outside, alone, at night, I keep
a vigil while the world's asleep;
alert to how bereft she is
I sing songs for her benefit,
laments for her unhappiness
expressing just how sad she is,
& for this show of sympathy
she warms to me & welcomes me.   1600
I strive to help such wives because
they seek to plot a noble course.
You've riled my heart to such a stage
it's almost paralyzed with rage
& I can barely speak a word,
but I'll continue, undeterred.
You say that I'm despised by men,
inspire hostility in them;
they threaten me with stones & sticks
then beat & smash my bones to bits   1610
& when all life in me is lost
they hang me from a hedge or post
to scare the magpie & the crow
in acres where the crops are sown.
And so, in truth, by shedding blood

an for heom ich [s]chadde mi blod:
ich do heom god mid mine deaþe,
waruore þe is wel unneaþe.
For þah þu ligge dead & clinge,
þi deþ nis nawt to none þinge: 1620
ich not neauer to hwan þu miȝt,
for þu nart bute a wrecche wiȝt.
Ah þah mi lif me beo atschote,
þe ȝet ich mai do gode note:
me mai up one smale sticke
me sette a-wude ine þe þicke,
an swa mai mon tolli him to
lutle briddes & iuo,
an swa me mai mid me biȝete
wel gode brede to his mete.   1630
Ah þu neure mon to gode
liues ne deaþes stal ne stode:
ich not to hwan þu bre[d]ist þi brod,
liues ne deaþes ne deþ hit god."

Þe nihtegale ih[e]rde þis,
an hupte uppon on blowe ris,
an herre sat þan heo dude ear:
"Hule," he seide, "beo nu wear,
nulle ich wiþ þe plaidi namore,
for her þe mist þi rihte lore: 1640
þu ȝeilpest þat þu art manne loþ,
an euereuch wiht is wið þe w[ro]þ;
an mid ȝulinge & mid igrede
þu wanst wel þat þu art unlede.

112

I'm helping out & doing good!
My death brings people benefit
which you find painful to admit,
for once you're shriveled up & gone
you are no use to anyone.   1620
Why you exist I just don't know
you good-for-nothing so-&-so,
but even when I cease to live
I still have something more to give:
when hunters mount me on a stick
in woods where trees grow dense & thick
I serve my purpose as a lure
for little birds, so I ensure
men have their share of roasted meat
by snaring food they like to eat.   1630
You're just as pointless when alert
as when you're lifeless & inert;
why bother bringing up a brood—
alive or dead they do no good."

The Nightingale took in this stance
then hopped up to a higher branch
& settled on a blossomed bough.
"Look, Owl," she said, "be careful now,
I won't react to you again
because all sense has left your brain.   1640
You boast that you infuriate,
that you're the object of man's hate,
& with that wailing, hooting blare
you wallow in your own despair.

113

Þu seist þat gromes þe ifoð,
an heie on rodde þe anhoð,
an þe totwichet & toschakeð,
an summe of þe schawles makeð.
Me þunc[þ] þat þu forleost þat game,
þu ʒulpest of þire oʒe schame: *1650*
me þunc[þ] þat þu me gest an honde,
þu ʒulpest of þire oʒene scho[nd]e."
Þo heo hadde þeos word icwede,
heo sat in ore faire stude,
an þarafter hire steuene dihte,
an song so schille & so brihte,
þat feor & ner me hit iherde.
Þaruore anan to hire cherde
þrusche & þrostle & wudewale,
an fuheles boþe grete & smale: *1660*
forþan heom þuhte þat heo hadde
þe houle ouercome, uorþan heo gradde
an sungen alswa uale wise,
an blisse was among þe rise.
Riʒt swa me gred þe manne a schame,
þat taueleþ & forleost þat gome.

Þeos hule, þo heo þis iherde,
"Hauestu," heo seide, "ibanned ferde?
an wultu, wreche, wið me fiʒte?
Nai! nai! nauestu none miʒte!   *1670*
Hwat gredeþ þeo þat hider come?
Me þuncþ þu ledest ferde to me.
ʒe schule wite, ar ʒe fleo heonne,

114

You say that lads set up their snares
then let you dangle in the air
& tear you limb from limb, or make
a scarecrow from you, on a stake.
It seems to me you've lost the game
by trumpeting your acts of shame;   *1650*
it seems that you concede the case
by glorifying your disgrace."
Once she had said her piece, she searched
& found a lovely place to perch
then tuned the workings of her throat
to find the most resounding notes
& sang so piercingly & clear
that birds flocked in from far & near,
the oriole & mistle thrush
& song thrush—big birds, small birds—rushed   *1660*
toward the scene on hearing that
the Nightingale had won the spat
& from the branches they gave voice
as if the trees themselves rejoiced,
& jeered the Owl, as if her vice
were gambling, & she'd lost at dice!

On hearing this the Owl replied:
"You've called an army to your side?
But do you really want to fight,
you stunted little featherweight?   *1670*
What are your allies shouting for?
If you propose to wage a war
you'll learn before you next take flight

hwuch is þe strenþe of mine kunne:
for þeo þe haueþ bile ihoked,
an cliures [s]charpe & wel icroked,
alle heo beoþ of mine kunrede,
an walde come ȝif ich bede.
Þe seolfe coc, þat wel can fiȝte,
he mot mid me holde mid riȝte,
for [boþe] we habbeþ steuene briȝte,
an sitteþ under weolcne bi niȝte.
Schille ich an utest uppen ow grede,
ich shal swo stronge ferde lede,
þat ower pr[u]de schal aualle:
a tort ne ȝiue ich for ow alle!
ne schal, ar hit beo fulliche eue,
a wreche feþer on ow bileaue.
Ah hit was unker uoreward,
þo we come hiderward,
þat we þarto holde scholde,
þar riht dom us ȝiue wolde.
Wultu nu breke foreward?
Ich wene dom þe þing[þ] to hard:
for þu ne darst domes abide,
þu wult nu, wreche, fiȝte & chide.
Ȝ[u]t ich ow alle wolde rede,
ar [ich] utheste uppon ow grede,
þat ower fihtlac leteþ beo,
an ginneþ raþe awei fleo.
For, bi þe cliures þat ich bere,
ȝef ȝe abideþ mine here,
ȝe schule on oþer wise singe,

116

what strength my family has, what might,
for all those enemies of yours
with curving beaks & pointed claws
are kin of mine, & if I send
for their assistance they'll attend,
among their ranks the fighting cock,
who would be right to cast his lot   1680
with me—we both have striking cries
& both sit under starry skies.
Were I to raise the battle cry
I'd rally so much infantry
your pride would fall to pieces, bird.
You & your kind aren't worth a turd,
& by the time the sun has set
you'll all be featherless. We met
with an agreement in this place
that fairness would decide our case,   1690
with honest rules to be observed
by which true justice would be served.
Now I suspect you'll break that pact;
you fear the verdict so you act
without fair judgment being reached,
& want to brawl instead, you wretch.
So I advise you—change your mind
before I cross the battle line;
be smart & quickly fly away
& live to fight another day.   1700
For if my legions mobilize
then by these talons that I prize
you'll sing a very different song

an acursi alle fiȝtinge:
vor nis of ow non so kene,
þat durre abide mine onsene."
Þeos hule spac wel baldeliche,
for þah heo nadde swo hwatliche
ifare after hire here,
heo walde neoþeles ȝefe answere   1710
þe niȝtegale mid swucche worde.
For moni man mid speres orde
haueþ lutle strencþe, & mid his [s]chelde,
ah neoþeles in one felde,
þurh belde worde an mid ilete,
deþ his iuo for arehþe swete.

Þe wranne, for heo cuþe singe,
þar com in þare moreȝcn[i]nge
to helpe þare niȝtegale:
for þah heo hadde steuene smale,   1720
heo hadde gode þ[ro]te & schille,
an fale manne song a wille.
Þe wranne was wel wis iholde,
vor þeȝ heo nere ibred a-wolde,
ho was itoȝen among man[k]enne,
an hire wisdom brohte þenne:
heo miȝte speke hwar heo walde,
touore þe king þah heo scholde.
"Lusteþ," heo cwaþ, "lateþ me speke.
Hwat! wulle ȝe þis pes tobreke,   1730
an do þanne [kinge] swuch schame?
Ȝe[t] nis he nouþer ded ne lame.

& curse all wars from this day on,
because not one of you can stare
me in the face—you wouldn't dare."
The Owl was forceful in her speech;
of course she hadn't yet beseeched
her troops to fight her cause, but railed
this way against the Nightingale   1710
for men have stood on battlefields
quite powerless, despite their shields,
despite the sharpness of their spears,
yet filled their enemies with fear
& caused their foes to quake & sweat
through warlike acts & hostile threats.

That morning, though, the wood had seen
the wren's arrival on the scene;
she'd come to help the Nightingale
because although her voice is small   1720
it rings out loud & sharp & clear
& brings enjoyment to the ear.
The wren's intelligence was praised;
that little bird had not been raised
in woods, but in the world of men,
& her astuteness came from them.
So she could sing out anywhere
(including if the king was there).
She said, "Now let me make my speech.
Do you intend to break the peace   1730
& put our royal king to shame
when he is neither dead nor lame?

Hunke schal itide harm & schonde,
ȝef ȝe doþ griþbruche on his londe.
Lateþ beo, & beoþ isome,
an fareþ riht to o[w]er dome,
an lateþ dom þis plaid tobreke,
al swo hit was erur bispeke."

"Ich an wel," cwað þe niȝtegale,
"ah, wranne, nawt for þire tale,
ah do for mire lahfulnesse.
Ich nolde þat unrihtfulnesse
me at þen ende ouerkome:
ich nam ofdrad of none dome.
Bihote ich habbe, soþ hit is,
þat Maister Nichole, þat is wis,
bituxen vs deme schul[l]e,
an ȝe[t] ich wene þat he wule.
Ah, [w]ar mihte we hine finde?"
Þe wranne sat in ore linde;
"Hwat! nu[s]te ȝe," cwaþ heo, "his hom?
He wuneþ at Porteshom,
at one tune ine Dorsete,
bi þare see in ore utlete:
þar he demeþ manie riȝte dom,
an diht & writ mani wisdom,
an þurh his muþe & þurh his honde
hit is þe betere into Scotlonde,
To seche hine is lihtlich þing;
he naueþ bute one woning.
Þat [is] bischopen muchel schame,

1740

1750

1760

You'll suffer harm & moral stain
by trading blows in his domain.
The two of you should call a truce
then go in search of rightful truth
& let a judgment be decreed,
as was initially agreed."

The Nightingale said, "Count me in.
Not out of deference to the wren   1740
but through my reverence for the law.
It wouldn't suit me if this score
was settled by injustice; I'll
be more than happy standing trial.
And yes, I promised to engage
that clever Simon Armitage
to take the role of magistrate—
& still have hopes he'll arbitrate,
but where shall we report to him?"
The wren, perched on a lime tree limb,   1750
said, "Don't you know?" And then revealed,
"He's domiciled near Huddersfield,
in Yorkshire, nowhere near the sea
& nowhere near an estuary.
That's where he lives, & in that town
he thinks wise thoughts & writes them down;
as far as Scotland life is better,
all because he's good with letters.
Finding him won't cause much strife,
he lives a solitary life,   1760
a shame for anyone who's heard

121

an alle [þ]an þat of his nome
habbeþ ihert, & of his dede.
Hwi nulleþ hi nimen heom to rede,
þat he were mid heom ilome
for teche heom of his wisdome,
an ȝiue him rente auale stude,
þat he miȝte heom ilome be mide?"

"Certes," cwaþ þe hule, "þat is soð:
þeos riche men wel muche misdoð,   *1770*
þat leteþ þane gode mon,
þat of so feole þinge con,
an ȝiueþ rente wel misliche,
an of him leteþ wel lihtliche.
Wið heore cunne heo beoþ mildre,
au ȝeueþ rente litle childre:
swo heore wit hi demþ adwole,
þut euer abid Maistre Nichole.
Ah ute we þah to him fare,
for þar is unker dom al ȝare."   *1780*

"Do we" þe niȝtegale seide:
"ah [w]a schal unker speche rede,
an telle touore unker deme?"

"Þarof ich schal þe wel icweme,"
cwaþ þe houle; "for al, ende of orde,
telle ich con, word after worde:
an ȝef þe þincþ þat ich misrempe,
þu stond aȝein & do me crempe."

122

the rumors of his crafted words
& stories of his clever deeds.
If bishops issued a decree
to share with him their revenues
& rents, then Armitage could choose
to venture from his residence
& reach a wider audience."

"Indeed that's true," the Owl exclaimed.
"Those wealthy men should be ashamed,   *1770*
not holding him in high regard,
not giving him his just reward,
a leading figure of his age.
And they are men who pay a wage
to family members, & who splash
substantial sums on little brats.
Neglecting Armitage so long
confirms their guilt & proves them wrong.
But come, let's find the one who'll bring
conclusion to our quarreling."   *1780*

The Nightingale said, "To his place
we'll go. But who'll present our case
& make submissions to him there?"

"In that department have no fear,"
the Owl replied. "All that was said
I memorized from A to Z,
& if you think I deviate
then intervene & put me straight."

Mid þisse worde forþ hi ferden,
al bute here & bute uerde,
1790
to Portesham þat heo bicome.
Ah hu heo spedde of heore dome,
ne [c]an ich eu namore telle:
her nis namore of þis spelle.

And with those words—without their troops
& followers—they took the route   1790
to Huddersfield, but what occurred
when claims & counterclaims were heard,
regrettably I can't relate—
here's where the poem terminates.

ACKNOWLEDGMENTS

Several excerpts from this translation originally appeared on the BBC Radio 4 program and podcast *The Poet Laureate Has Gone to His Shed.*

A facsimile edition of both original manuscripts of the poem, published by Oxford University Press for The Early English Text Society (1963), has been both a valuable companion and a totemic presence on my desk for the past three years or so. The definitive critical edition is Neil Cartlidge's *The Owl and the Nightingale* (Liverpool University Press, 2016; first published 2001 by University of Exeter Press). That transcription and translation, including a comprehensive analysis, appendices, notes, bibliography, and glossary is indispensable to any student of the poem; I am indebted to its scholarship and grateful for its existence. Brian Stone's translation (Penguin Classics, 1988) also contains an invaluable commentary on the poem, especially in relation to its biblical and theological underpinnings. I have also drawn on transcriptions by Eric Gerald Stanley (Manchester University Press, 1981), J.W.H. Atkins (Cambridge University Press, 1922), and John Edwin Wells (D.C. Heath and Co., 1907). There are now innumerable internet resources dedicated to the transmission and translation of the poem, including Wessex Parallel Web Texts and the Corpus of Middle

English Prose and Verse, often with dedicated glossaries or providing access to dictionaries of Middle English. I am grateful to all those academic institutions who have made their work on the poem available to visiting researchers, especially those granting public online access.

The facing-page Middle English text in this volume is drawn from "The Owl and the Nightingale" (MS Cotton), Corpus of Middle English Prose and Verse, University of Michigan Text Initiative, quod.lib.umich.edu/c/cme/OwlC.

The Lockert Library of Poetry in Translation

George Seferis: Collected Poems, 1924–1955, translated, edited, and introduced by Edmund Keeley and Philip Sherrard
Collected Poems of Lucio Piccolo, translated and edited by Brian Swann and Ruth Feldman
C. P. Cavafy: Collected Poems, translated by Edmund Kelley and Philip Sherrard and edited by George Savidis
Benny Andersen: Selected Poems, translated by Alexander Taylor
Selected Poetry of Andrea Zanzotto, edited and translated by Ruth Feldman and Brian Swann
Poems of René Char, translated and annotated by Mary Ann Caws and Jonathan Griffin⁺
Selected Poems of Tudor Arghezi, translated by Michael Impey and Brian Swann
"The Survivor" and Other Poems, by Tadeusz Różewicz, translated and introduced by Magnus J. Krynski and Robert A. Maguire
"Harsh World" and Other Poems, by Angel González, translated by Donald D. Walsh
Ritsos in Parentheses, translated and introduced by Edmund Keeley
Salamander: Selected Poems of Robert Marteau, translated by Anne Winters
Angelos Sikelianos: Selected Poems, translated and introduced by Edmund Keeley and Philip Sherrard⁺
Dante's "Rime," translated by Patrick S. Diehl
Selected Later Poems of Marie Luise Kaschnitz, translated by Lisel Mueller
Osip Mandelstam's "Stone," translated and introduced by Robert Tracy⁺
The Dawn Is Always New: Selected Poetry of Rocco Scotellaro, translated by Ruth Feldman and Brian Swann
Sounds, Feelings, Thoughts: Seventy Poems by Wisława Szymborska, translated and introduced by Magnus J. Krynski and Robert A. Maguire
George Seferis: Collected Poems, 1924–1955, Expanded Edition [bilingual], translated, edited, and introduced by Edmund Keeley and Philip Sherrard
The Man I Pretend to Be: "The Colloquies" and Selected Poems of Guido Gozzano, translated and edited by Michael Palma, with an introductory essay by Eugenio Montale
D'Après Tout: Poems by Jean Follain, translated by Heather McHugh⁺
Songs of Something Else: Selected Poems of Gunnar Ekelöf, translated by Leonard Nathan and James Larson

The Little Treasury of One Hundred People, One Poem Each, compiled by Fujiwara No Sadaie and translated by Tom Galt[+]

The Ellipse: Selected Poems of Leonardo Sinisgalli, translated by W. S. Di Pietro[+]

The Difficult Days, by Roberto Sosa, translated by Jim Lindsey

Hymns and Fragments, by Friedrich Hölderin, translated and introduced by Richard Sieburth

The Silence Afterwards: Selected Poems of Rolf Jacobsen, translated and edited by Roger Greenwald[+]

Rilke: Between Roots, selected poems rendered from the German by Rika Lesser[+]

In the Storm of Roses: Selected Poems, by Ingeborg Bachmann, translated, edited, and introduced by Mark Anderson[+]

Birds and Other Relations: Selected Poetry of Dezső Tandori, translated by Bruce Berlind

Brocade River Poems: Selected Works of the Tang Dynasty Courtesan Xue Tao, translated and introduced by Jeanne Larsen

The True Subject: Selected Poems of Faiz Ahmed Faiz, translated by Naomi Lazard

My Name on the Wind: Selected Poems of Diego Valeri, translated by Michael Palma

Aeschylus: The Suppliants, translated by Peter Burian

C. P. Cavafy: Collected Poems, Revised Edition, translated and introduced by Edmund Keeley and Philip Sherrard, edited by George Savidis

Foamy Sky: The Major Poems of Miklós Radnóti, selected and translated by Zsuzsanna Ozsváth and Frederick Turner[+]

La Fontaine's Bawdy: Of Libertines, Louts, and Lechers, translated by Norman R. Shapiro[+]

A Child Is Not a Knife: Selected Poems of Göran Sonnevi, translated and edited by Rika Lesser

George Seferis: Collected Poems, Revised Edition [English only], translated, edited, and introduced by Edmund Keeley and Philip Sherrard

Selected Poems of Shmuel HaNagid, translated by Peter Cole

The Late Poems of Meng Chiao, translated by David Hinton

Leopardi: Selected Poems, translated and introduced by Eamon Grennan

Through Naked Branches: Selected Poems of Tarjei Vesaas, translated and edited by Roger Greenwald[+]

The Complete Odes and Satires of Horace, translated with introduction and notes by Sidney Alexander

Selected Poems of Solomon Ibn Gabirol, translated by Peter Cole

Puerilities: Erotic Epigrams of "The Greek Anthology," translated by Daryl Hine

Night Journey, by María Negroni, translated by Anne Twitty
*The Poetess Counts to 100 and Bows Out: Selected Poems by Ana
Enriqueta Terán*, translated by Marcel Smith
Nothing Is Lost: Selected Poems, by Edvard Kocbek, translated by
Michael Scammell and Veno Taufer, and introduced by Michael
Scammell, with a foreword by Charles Simic
The Complete Elegies of Sextus Propertius, translated with introduction
and notes by Vincent Katz
Knowing the East, by Paul Claudel, translated with introduction and
notes by James Lawler
Enough to Say It's Far: Selected Poems of Pak Chaesam, translated by
David R. McCann and Jiwon Shin
In Hora Mortis / Under the Iron of the Moon: Poems, by Thomas
Bernhard, translated by James Reidel
The Greener Meadow: Selected Poems, by Luciano Erba, translated by
Peter Robinson
*The Dream of the Poem: Hebrew Poetry from Muslim and Christian Spain,
950–1492*, translated, edited, and introduced by Peter Cole
The Collected Lyric Poems of Luís de Camões, translated by Landeg White
C. P. Cavafy: Collected Poems, Bilingual Edition, translated by Edmund
Keeley and Philip Sherrard, edited by George Savidis, with a new
preface by Robert Pinsky
Poems under Saturn: Poèmes saturniens, by Paul Verlaine, translated and
with an introduction by Karl Kirchwey
Final Matters: Selected Poems, 2004–2010, by Szilárd Borbély, translated
by Ottilie Mulzet
Selected Poems of Giovanni Pascoli, translated by Taije Silverman with
Marina Della Putta Johnston
After Callimachus: Poems, by Stephanie Burt, with a foreword by Mark
Payne
Dear Ms. Schubert: Poems by Ewa Lipska, translated by Robin
Davidson and Ewa Elżbieta Nowakowska, with a foreword by Adam
Zagajewski
The Translator of Desires, by Muhyiddin Ibn 'Arabi, translated by Michael
Sells
Cantigas: Galician-Portuguese Troubadour Poems, translated and
introduced by Richard Zenith
The Owl and the Nightingale: A New Verse Translation, translated by
Simon Armitage

† Out of print

www.ingramcontent.com/pod-product-compliance
Lightning Source LLC
Jackson TN
JSHW080203141224
75386JS00029B/1015